EVOLUTION FOR EVERYONE

The Science and Society Series

This series of books, under the general editorship of the Biological Sciences Curriculum Study (BSCS), is for people who have both an interest in biology and a continuing desire to teach themselves. The books are short, highly readable, and nontechnical; each is written by a specialist on a particular, significant aspect of biology. Consistent with a long-standing premise of BSCS, the authors approach their topics as a base for inquiry; they pose questions and help the reader to see the way a scientist arrives at answers or where answers are to be sought. While the books are oriented for the layman primarily, it is hoped that they will also prove useful to high school and college students who wish more background in unfamiliar fields.

There are two major types of books in the series. One of these is directed to the continued and practical problems of society for which biology has both information and a message; topics such as birth control, eugenics and drugs are of personal interest and concern to most individuals. The other cluster of books is devoted to the continuing problems of biology; these topics, such as animal behavior, population biology, and chemical coordination, often relate to societal problems and are of particular concern to biology as a developing discipline. Together, the two clusters give some measure of the totality of modern biology, to which we invite your time and attention.

William V. Mayer
Director, BSCS
Boulder, Colorado

EVOLUTION
FOR
EVERYONE

✳✳✳

Paul R. Gastonguay

A Biological Sciences Curriculum Study Book

Pegasus

A DIVISION OF

The Bobbs-Merrill Company, Inc., Publishers

INDIANAPOLIS   NEW YORK

Library of Congress Cataloging in Publication Data

Gastonguay, Paul R.   1936–
  Evolution for everyone.

  (The Science and society series)
  "A Biological Sciences Curriculum Study Book."
  Bibliography: p.
  1. Evolution.   I. Title.
  QH367.G344   575   73–5809
  ISBN 0–672–53712–5
  ISBN 0–672–63712–X (pbk.)

A writer merely thinks and pens.

A wife must
        brighten, enlighten,
        console, condole,
        leave alone, eat alone,
        shovel, shop, and feed the hens.

To my wife.

Acknowledgments

The author and publisher are grateful to the following for permission to reprint.

Figure 2: G. E. Nelson, et al., *Fundamental Concepts of Biology*, 2nd ed. Copyright 1970 by John Wiley & Sons, Inc. Reprinted by permission.

Figure 3: "Differentiation in Social Amoeba" by John Tyler Bonner. Copyright © December 1959 by Scientific American, Inc. All rights reserved.

Figures 4A and *4B:* "The Breakup of Pangaea" by Robert S. Dietz and John C. Holden. Copyright © October 1970 by Scientific American, Inc. All rights reserved.

Figure 5: Bryce Canyon National Park, U.S.D.I., National Park Service Photo.

Figure 8: From *A Manual of Aquatic Plants* by N. C. Fassett. Copyright 1940 by McGraw-Hill, Inc. Used by permission of McGraw-Hill Book Company.

Figure 9: Bruce Wallace and Adrian M. Srb, *Adaptation,*

2nd ed., © 1964. Reprinted by permission of Prentice-Hall, Inc., Englewood Cliffs, New Jersey.

Figure 10: From the experiments of Dr. H. B. D. Kettlewell, Oxford University.

Figure 11: From *Mimicry in Plants and Animals* by W. Wickles. Drawing by H. Kacker.

Figure 25A: From Guyer, *Animal Biology* (1948). By permission of Harper & Row.

Figure 25B: By permission of American Society of Mammalogists.

Figure 26: Courtesy of Joseph Muench.

Figure 27: Courtesy of W. C. Bradley.

Figure 32: Courtesy of Stuart A. Altmann, University of Chicago.

All other figures courtesy of the *Biological Sciences Curriculum Study*, Boulder, Colorado.

Editor's Preface

"You've come a long way, baby," goes a popular advertising slogan. It goes for what has happened in the natural world. Our own galaxy of stars has come a long way from its initial compactness of stellar dust; our present continents and oceans have come a long way from their initial one continent–one ocean ancestor; and modern man has come a long way from his primate ancestors and an even longer way from the initial organic soup.

Stars, land, and man—all part of the inexorable and inescapable process of change, of evolution. Evolution: a process occurring over an immensity of time few of us are able to comprehend. Paul Gastonguay has written an easily understood account of these evolutionary events and of the processes which have brought man and matter to their present state.

There is an inherent basis for interest in stars, land, and man—we are so much a part of them, inextricably interwoven in the very fabric of nature. But, today, there are more compelling reasons why we need to know about the processes that have brought us to our current evolutionary state, why we need to understand man's place in the nature of things. We have moved without fanfare into a period of biological manipulation, of mind altering/controlling drugs, surgical replacement of defunct organs, and the like. Biological manipulation includes test-tube babies, genetic surgery, sperm and egg banks—the very ingredients of the potential for engineering the course of man's future evolution.

Do we know where we want to go? Do we know how we can get there? Do we know what the hazards are in getting there? These are some of the questions for which Mr. Gastonguay's book prepares us. If it is followed by a reading of other books in this BSCS Science and Society Series, especially E. Peter Volpe's HUMAN HEREDITY AND BIRTH DEFECTS, a reader will have a good initial grasp on what potentials and problems lie ahead in human evolution.

Edward J. Kormondy
Olympia, Washington

Contents

Man the Prosecutor

*

LAW AND ORDER

I

The First Chapter

Have you ever seen an old washing machine adorning a neighbor's lawn? It is a pitiful sight indeed as it pouts there, probably rusting, and overpopulated with flowers, weeds, and vines. It cannot help but cause the gentle flow of tears from the mind of a sentimentalist.

I am a sentimentalist.

And as I view such a dismal display of outright squandering, the long history of this poor washed-up tub spans my imagination. I strain a backward glance at its parents, and their parents, and theirs. And thus do I become aware of the awe-inspiring ancestry that is now evaporating from this fading-yellow, scrubbed tub.

A marvelous species of Thing, the washing machine. At one time it possessed a wringer, occasionally a crank, and in noise could outwit any Model T. But as it aged it gave birth to countless offspring. Thus grew a hereditary lineage by which this Thing has become as functional and as beautiful as it is today. It deserves our highest esteem.

Yes indeed—the washing machine has evolved. The pitiful tub that now rests on my neighbor's lawn has been replaced by streamlined, decorative, highly functional, diminutive washing machines, each snugly embraced by the mod housewife's Formica-topped washroom counters.

The point of this opening is this: here is a machine, a mass of parts whose relationships and whose functions have been multiplied and improved at the hands of human beings who seemingly learn more and more with each passing generation, each succeeding flock being a little wiser than its parents.

And so have evolved also the automobile, the can opener, eyeglasses, highway systems, television sets, and screwdrivers.

Such are the changes, the improvements, the adaptations to modern times, which the human species can produce. Everything seems to change. Many things seem to change for the better. Sometimes man causes the change; sometimes nature does. If the change occurs naturally, and in living things, we call it "biological evolution." If it occurs artificially, and in such things as machines and roads, we call it "progress." Perhaps it is merely a matter of semantics; but perhaps not.

However, it is fascinating that, as complicated and as powerful as man's inventions appear, they represent only a minute fraction of Mother Nature's complexities and powers.

The Power of Nature

Powerful are the forces that control the tides, the Earth's orbit, the flow of starlight to your eyes, or your brain's interpretation of what your eyes see. There is much in nature, "out there" and "in here," over which man has no control. So many forces—so much power which we cannot yet fully explain: a sodium atom falling in love with a chlorine atom and presto—table salt; sugar losing its personal identity in hot coffee; a sun rising. There is also so much of our own biology that we cannot control, or that we do without thinking: a musician tapping his foot instinctively; tears that come when an author receives a rejection notice; tears that accompany a child's fall; sneezing, coughing, yawning, blushing, shivering; falling asleep; retreating from a hot iron; even responding emotionally in anger, fear, or love. The movements of both tears and oceans can occur whether you like it or not.

As you view an immense quantity of water shifting toward you for ten or twenty feet along an ocean beach, you might report passively, perhaps yawning, "the tide is in." But can you imagine, for a moment, the immense powers that are causing what you have just witnessed? At first it all makes the Man Thing, the Washing Machine Engineer, the crying animal, look rather inconsequential.

Man: Animal, Computer, Etc.

The Man Thing. Man the Engineer. Man the animal. Surely everyone should agree that man has some animal nature in him. It is a beautifully complex animal nature, with elusive instincts, elaborate behavior patterns, and valuable traditions, but it is nevertheless animal; the most able of animal natures.

And we should realize that man is also a computer; a computer that can program itself; a complex chemistry able to guide itself to do what it wishes, to somehow overcome the natural, instinctive response built into it. Whatever man is psychologically, sociologically, spiritually, or philosophically, he is certainly also biological. We

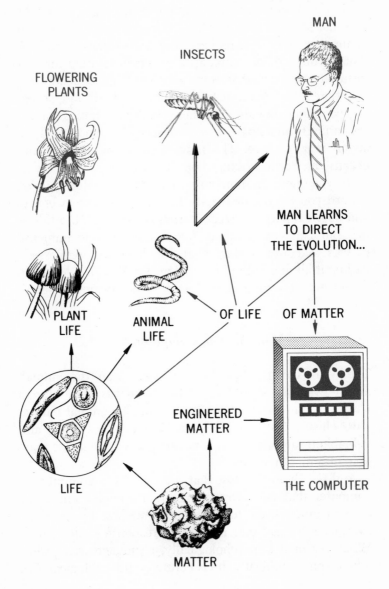

will here, in this book, analyze mainly the *biology* of man.

Man is uniquely able to outwit nature. When he cannot see, he wears glasses; when he cannot hear, he wears a hearing aid. He has artificial limbs, crutches, wigs, and artificial organs. And perhaps the smiles are synthetic, plastic or gold, bought from the dentist. He reshapes his nose, deodorizes his sweat, lengthens his eyebrows, paints his face, replaces his heart, and fattens his breasts. He has cars to assist legs, computers to assist brains, and test tubes to assist wombs. He has learned to modify his emotions with drugs and to affect his personality by psychiatry or hormones, or by cutting the appropriate nerve.

Man the animal. Man the computer. Man the Thing. But a very biologically superior Thing. He is now the star of the show; the discoverer, the analyzer, the instigator of future shows. This then makes his the most trouble-making and unpopular role on Earth. But he is not alone on stage. He has powerful competitors. True, he is the most highly complex Thing, but only so in his own line of ancestry. There are now, and there were in the past, other Things also highly complicated, at the peaks of their ancestries. Today's peaks, besides man, include the insects, the flowering plants, and man's inventions; we can classify the last group as "engineered matter." The relative positions of these four peaks are illustrated in Figure 1.

Figure 1. Path along which some material substances diverged into living things and "engineered matter." In part, life has yielded plants and animals, the most advanced of which are flowering plants, insects, and man. The computer is presently the most complex "engineered matter." Man himself can now control much of the evolution process.

A Cell, A Society: Where to Draw the Line?

It is not solely at the peaks of the four lines of "Thing development," or evolution, that we see confusion and marvel. Lower forms of life display a maze of confusing activities, and of powerful abilities, as well. In fact, it is often by analyzing the lower forms of life that we learn of past happenings on our Earth, that we learn of the origin and true significance of man.

For example, have you ever seen an ameba? You would need a microscope; it is one of many kinds of one-celled

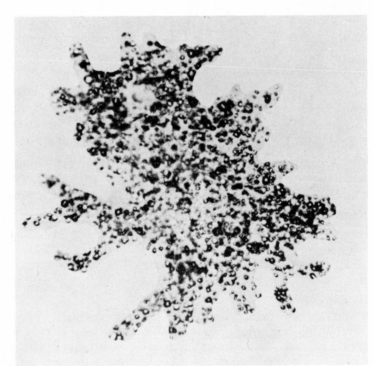

Figure 2. An ameba in motion.

animals. Your own body is made up of ten trillion cells each more or less the size of one ameba. (See Figure 2.) The fascinating thing about the ameba is not its size, but what it can do with its one cell. It can eat, reproduce, move, and *cause itself* to do some of these things. It has the heredity, the code, to initiate some of its actions, when stimulated to do so. For lack of a larger English vocabulary, we must say that it truly can tell itself to do some things. Something in it and controlled by it tells it to do something. That is quite an achievement for one cell!

The ameba moves about by extending parts of itself outward, to form finger-like extensions; some of our own body's cells can do the same thing, moving through our tissues as if they were independent of our body. There is also a third kind of cell, besides the ameba and some of our cells, that can move in a similar manner; some kinds of molds, called *social amebas,* move ameba-fashion.

The social ameba is not an ameba, but a mold; it bears the name of the ameba merely because of its resemblance to it. But the social ameba does a very strange thing at times. Although remarkably self-sufficient as single cells, like true amebas, sometimes a large number of social amebas, as many as 100,000, congregate into one area, then move off together as a team to form a large society. Later on, some of the cells begin to form a stem, some form a base for support, and still another group of cells find their way to the top of the rising stem. As this last group of cells becomes situated atop the stem, they lose most of their previous abilities. Instead, they become specialized in one important activity: reproduction of the species. (See Figure 3.)

Therefore, in a kind of plant so small that each cell must contain everything needed to survive the cold and threatening waters, we find that a large number of these cells aggregate to form a many-celled organism (or a

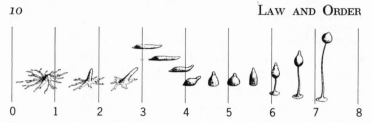

Figure 3. Aggregation of single cells of a slime mold into a multi-celled body.

society—take your pick) for one purpose: reproduction. Somewhere along the line the social ameba has lost, or never gained, the ability of individual cell reproduction. The cells can survive alone, but they cannot reproduce alone. The only recourse, then, has been to find another way to continue the existence of the species. Such a way was found. The species evolved to form a very simple, primitive society with all members sharing in the process of survival and continuation. Some members form only the supporting structure, some only the stem, and some become solely reproductive cells. The spores that are released from the latter cells become new "baby" mold cells, each going off on its own until such time as reproduction again becomes the order of the day.

But is it justifiable to call this adaptation an evolution?

Evolution Defined—Almost

Evolution. Everyone has heard the word. Everyone has his own idea of its meaning. Quite unfortunately, to some it has only one narrow meaning. They associate one word with evolution; that word is "ape." But there is so much more.

Surprisingly, some educated men very unrealistically reject evolution without extensive reading in the area—and sometimes apparently with no reading at all. They fail to realize that there is no factual knowledge to which anyone can refer for the purpose of denying evolution. Some who do not bother to maintain an acquaintance with scientific discoveries would realize, if they did so, that there is a great deal of positive information to substantiate the belief that evolution permeates every last bit of existence.

All sorts of things, of all sizes, evolve: everything from large clusters of stars to our sun, to the Earth, its oceans, atmosphere, continents, and mountains; to babies and crying and language and screwdrivers and knitting needles; the evolution of hydrogen gas into everything that exists, including life itself. The processes are somewhat different for objects of different sizes and complexities, but the overall outcome of evolution is always the same—improvement.

Why I Wrote This Book

In the book you are now reading, you will find no extensive arguments that attempt to prove the occurrence of an evolution. It is not my purpose here to enter into debate on the issue. The reader can simply acquire copies of some of the books listed in the back of this book, and see for himself the evidence advanced in defense of evolution. There are countless worthwhile books describing, teaching, the evolutionary process. My intention here is not so much to teach as to clarify what has been taught.

When the vast majority of skilled men agree on something, a rare event indeed, one must surely be cautious in rejecting their joint opinion. When men of science, philosophy, and sociology confirm the findings that have elevated evolution to a "law" of nature in the minds of most men, when no scientific discovery denies that evolution has occurred, it seems futile indeed simply to reject evolution without proper training, observation, or reading. And yet, it is being done.

I must assume that the reader is prepared to be objective, to read this book without being defensive. This will allow me a greater opportunity to explain how the process of evolution occurs in five categories of Things: (1) stars, (2) the crust of our Earth, (3) the Earth's living things, collectively referred to as the *biosphere*, (4) man, and (5) human tools and products, especially as applied to medicine, the New Biology, and genetic engineering. Evolution can thus be analyzed astronomically, geologically, biologically, anthropologically, and technologically.

Evolution is not restricted to living things, except when evolution is narrowly defined. It is a phenomenon that surpasses, and to some extent guides, all others. Therefore, a survey of evolution must touch upon all levels of Things, whether living or not.

Another reason for writing this book is that the world is on the verge of a violent biological revolution. It must be obvious as one reads *The Biological Time Bomb* (G. Taylor), *Utopian Motherhood* (R. Francoeur), *Biocrats* (G. Leach), and *Bodies in Revolt* (T. Hanna), that this could become one of the most dramatic and potentially perilous revolutions that the Earth has ever seen. The last chapter will survey some of these aspects.

Suffice it to say here that because Mother Nature has yielded to man as the highest thinker, this same nature, now called Human Nature, is becoming able to change much of what has already been formed, to manipulate future evolution as he desires. This concept is illustrated in Figure 1. Awareness of this possibility is essential for all of us who wish to survive the psychological tremors that genetics and some of the other biological sciences will create, possibly in the near future.

Escape will be impossible. Knowledge will be the first requirement for survival, psychological survival. In accordance with my belief that all laymen must soon become acquainted with the New Biology, one of the areas of acquaintance must be the evolutionary process. If man does not know his position in the history of the biosphere, as well as his present and possible future roles, then man might not survive the explosion of biologic manipulation and the reorganizations that will follow in sociology and ethics.

When we can change moods, attitudes, and personalities, when we can produce babies in test tubes, when we can prolong an old man's life forever, then it will be too late to say: "But I never expected these things to be fulfilled." The fluoridation and abortion issues of the 1960s and 1970s will be as firecrackers compared to the mass bombings of biological change.

II

A Universe Is Acting Up

Should you be fortunate enough to have had the time to peacefully scan the heavens some evening, you should have realized that some of the starlight you were viewing began its journey of 9,000,000,000,000,000,000 miles some 1½ million years ago; and that you were literally seeing 1½ million years into the past. With the best telescopes, you could have been glancing backward even further, over 2 billion years.

The numbers and distances of stars and of planets in the universe do not mean much to most of us. When there are so many of one thing that we cannot count them, cannot see them, cannot even imagine them, then numbers become merged in a fog of confusion. When I am told that 77 billion human babies have been separated from their umbilical cords since man arrived on this planet, I could just as well be told 7 billion. Both numbers would ring the same bell in my mind. I would simply shrug both off as being "many" babies. Yet one number is eleven times as great as the other. Imagine your town with eleven times its present population; or your household.

So numbers may not mean much to us, but they certainly do influence the things being counted. Whether starlight travels at 186,000 miles per second or at 18,600 miles per second (the first is correct) may be quite meaningless to me, but not to one who studies the physics of starlight.

This is undoubtedly true of cosmic numbers in general. Each number is quite crucial for the proper operations of our universe. But still human nature prevails, and when the astronomer tells us that perhaps 1000 trillion galaxies exist in the universe, all you and I might wish to accept is that there are "many." I have compiled some "manies" in Table 1 and have added some cosmic distances and diameters. Also in the Table are some ages—how long ago some of the key events in our history occurred. Some of the numbers represent guesses, while others are rather well substantiated. The guesses are marked by asterisks.

A COSMIC ACCOUNT

Numbers

*Galaxies in the Universe	1 000 000 000 000 000
Galaxies visible to us (telescope)	1 000 000 000
*Stars in the Universe	100 000 000 000 000 000 000
Stars in our galaxy—the Milky Way	100 000 000 000
Stars visible to us (naked eye)	10 000

Distances (miles)

Earth to nearest galaxy	900 000 000 000 000 000
Earth to nearest star	26 000 000 000 000
Earth to Sun	93 000 000
Earth to Moon	239 000
Washington, D.C., to Peking, China	6 922

Diameters (miles)

*Universe	150 000 000 000 000 000 000 000
Milky Way	600 000 000 000 000 000
Sun	864 000
Earth	7 918

Times (years ago)

*Universe originates	15 000 000 000
Milky Way originates	10 000 000 000
Starlight of 1973 leaves farthest visible galaxy	5 000 000 000
Earth originates	4 800 000 000
Life originates on Earth	3 000 000 000
Continents form	65 000 000
Early Man originates	2 000 000
Modern Man originates	40 000
First known inhabitants of North America	13 000
Leif Ericsson discovers America	973
Charles Darwin publishes *Origin of Species*	114

My goal, however, is to constrict your mind, to narrow its focus from the "many" to our own local galaxy, the Milky Way. Then I will attempt to create some even more narrow-minded readers by focusing on our Earth, this beautiful and fortunate planet. Fortunate because you and I abide here, I suppose. But although I wish to look at the evolution of life here at home, to do so without first knowing where *home* fits into the universal scheme is to deceive and shortchange you.

The point of course is that our one tiny planet should indeed suffer an astronomical inferiority complex, in the light of its being only one of so "many" universal planets.

Hence, before coming home, let us look at the sky a bit longer. The "sky"—the universe—is said to be expanding; so goes the theory. For example, some stars are believed to be moving away from us at the incredible speed of 15,000 miles per second. The universe could be expanding because new matter is constantly being added to it, possibly by the continuous conversion of energy into matter. Such new materials could cause the older materials to move on. Or it could be expanding because of a massive explosion of some 10 to 20 billion years ago, in what has been referred to as the "Big Bang." Presently the balance is shifting toward the Big Bang theory.

Moreover, there is the possibility that there may have occurred repeated Big Bangs. This can be referred to as a Universal Oscillation theory. The theory assumes that a Big Bang would provide the exploding particles with just so much momentum, just so much "drive." These particles would then move out under the influence of this momentum. But the particles simultaneously would be attracted to each other by the force of gravity. Once the latter force overcomes the former, once the braking action exceeds the drive, there could result a universal "slowing down," then a contraction, with all particles returning to the site of the previous explosion. In this condensed ball of universal stuff, there would then be generated unbelievable forces, causing another Big Bang. And the process would repeat over and over again.

Those that subscribe to this theory estimate that the total cycle would require 82 billion years; 41 for expansion, 41 for contraction. We would then be about 15 billion years into the present expansion.

A Star Is Born

When a group of particles is dispersing, when the particles are moving away from one another, one could say that the *density* of the particles is decreasing. Look at it this way. If 1,000 kids simultaneously release their balloons at a Saturday afternoon parade, at first the balloons are crowded together as they rise above the heads of angry daddies. But once the balloons reach rooftop level, they are more dispersed; their density has decreased. Imagine that the universal particles do the same thing, after a Big Bang.

One theory that attempts to explain how galaxies and stars form suggests that the Milky Way began to isolate itself from the rest of universal stuff shortly after the Big Bang. Prior to this time, all particles had too much energy and "refused" to merge with other particles. But once the appropriate density was reached, things could begin to attract each other and to condense. Gravity, the force that attracts celestial bodies to each other, could now become effective. This might be the time when our Milky Way began to condense.

Conceivably, if the stuff presently making up our galaxy had not condensed at that particular time, at that "ideal" density of particles, it would not have merged at all. Later on the particles would have spread still further apart, too distant from each other for gravity to attract them. And the Milky Way would never have formed.

Within this forming galaxy many stars condensed. One was our sun, which eventually came to support nine planets and over fifty other smaller satellites. This occurred off to one rim of the flat cartwheel—that is what the Milky Way looks like—600,000 trillion miles across.

Our sun is one small star out of 100 billion others in our galaxy alone. There I go again with numbers.

However, the whole thing becomes rather confusing at times. Just when we think that we have theories and numbers to fit everything, an astronomer discovers the quasar. So what is a quasar, and why is it a problem to us? Well, some quasars can emit as much radiation as 1,000 galaxies! We are unable to explain how this much energy can come from a massive explosion somewhere out there, in a region less than one percent the size of our solar system; one small bit of space bombarding us with as much radiation as could be produced by 1,000 galaxies.

Bothersome as quasars are, however, we must continue our search for explanations. We must come to be able to map the heavens, and their activities, if we are to fully understand the sequence of events that made possible the evolution of that Thing called man; the only Thing that can see its reflection upon stars, and enjoy it.

Not only do we know a great deal about the evolution of galaxies, but of stars as well. We know that stars have a "life cycle," a predictable series of developments whereby a star is born, matures, ages, and dies. After it has exhausted its fuel supply, it faces one of several end stages, depending partly on its size. I urge you to further your reading in this fascinating subject of stellar old age and death.

Let us end this section by speculating. It has been estimated that the Milky Way alone could contain 600 million to 3 billion planets with conditions suitable for life on them. If the estimate should be ninety-nine percent wrong, that could still mean 6 million planets with possible life of any sort, probably mostly microscopic life. It has also been estimated that 3,000 planets in the Milky Way could now be supporting human life. On the average, that could place us 6,000 trillion miles away from our nearest cousins!

III

A Planet in Motion

Our Earth was formed about 4.8 billion years ago. According to the Continental Drift Theory, which is becoming increasingly accepted, it is presumed that millions of years ago all the surface land on the planet was concentrated in one massive continent, called *Pangaea*. It occupied forty percent of the Earth's surface, says the theory. New York City real estate would have been near the Equator at that time.

If the theory is correct, then the existence of one huge landmass means that there was one huge water mass. This original ocean is now called the Pacific Ocean. The other oceans were formed by the splitting and moving of continents; the exposed areas subsequently filled with water.

Figure 4-A is a map of the world as if it were flattened out. It illustrates Pangaea as it might have looked 200 million years ago. The solid horizontal line represents the Equator, and the dotted lines inside Pangaea represent

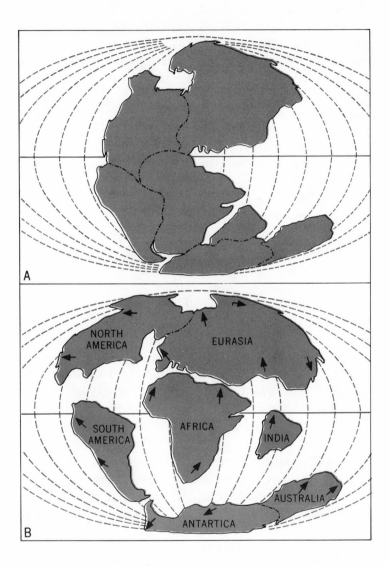

Figure 4A. The Earth's land mass 200 million years ago.
Figure 4B. The continents as presumed to have migrated by 65 million years ago.

the regions where this landmass eventually split into the present continents. Some smaller areas of land that exist today, besides the continents, are not marked off inside this map of Pangaea, even if they too originated from it.

It is theorized that 200 million years ago Pangaea began to split into two separate supercontinents, Laurasia above the Equator, and Gondwana to the south. This fragmentation was largely completed by 135 million years ago. At that time, the two supercontinents themselves began to split, and by 65 million years ago the present continents were formed.

Figure 4-B shows the positions of the continents, some still not entirely separated, 65 million years ago. The arrows represent the directions of Earth crust movements within each continent; they also indicate the directions of distortion within continents. Notice for example how the North American continent changed its outline, from the time of Figure 4-A to that of Figure 4-B. Some smaller land areas are not shown on the latter figure.

It is presumed that the continents have floated ever since their origin, and are still moving today. If you are seventy years old, you can boast that the North American continent has moved farther west, since you were born, by about the length of your body. Most Pangaea "pieces" have drifted westward, because of the direction of the Earth's spin.

According to the theory, the Indian subcontinent has made the longest migration of all the drifting land plates. After divorcing itself from Antarctica, it moved some 5,600 miles. Interestingly, when India reached the southeast corner of the Eurasian continent, the "worlds collided," and India slid under Asia a bit, creating an upheaval called the Himalayas.

If the theory is correct, then it is interesting that about 165 million years ago, when reptiles ruled the Earth, our

planet's land was still concentrated into two supercontinents. Subsequently, as reptiles gave rise to a line leading
to mammals, the primitive mammals had just barely
enough time to spread to all corners of the two huge landmasses before the latter split into today's several continents. The fragmentation of the supercontinents isolated
some mammal groups from others—an event that had immense repercussions in the future evolution of life.

Plates Across the Sea

As you bathe in ocean waters on a Sunday afternoon, do
not expect to see a continent drifting by. The continents
are parts of huge deep plates whose movements are very
slow because they are related to movements of the Earth's
entire crust.

The crust of our planet is twelve to thirty miles thick;
and it has the remarkable ability to heal itself, as our skin
does. For example, it has been able to heal the impact
wounds from the large meteors that bombarded the Earth
after its origin. The moon has no such ability, hence we
see all those moon craters.

The hard crust of the Earth slides rather easily over
the hard mantle beneath. Therefore, a soft layer of material may be between these two—one is tempted to say
a "jelly-like" layer. Some investigators believe that there
is. They call it the asthenosphere, or rheosphere, and presume that it is some 60 to 250 miles thick.

Now, try to imagine an Earth once fiery hot, later cooling, then land appearing. The land splits, and the fragments migrate, as huge plates of crust material are pulled
away from each other. Continents drift. Imagine also that
the flexibility of the crust is not confined to land areas, but
to the ocean floors as well. After all, if landmasses can

be affected by shifts in the crust, so can ocean floors. The two are part of the crust, and form a continuum.

The theory of Sea Floor Spreading, which we have just slid into, holds that the oceans are now expanding by more than six inches each year in some areas. At this rate the Earth would have had enough time to produce, in succession, forty Pacific Oceans; we would now be bathing in Pacific Ocean Number Forty. The North Atlantic Ocean has been enlarging at a constant rate of nearly one-half inch per year during the past 80 million years. It is not that the oceans are "filling up" with water, but they are actually expanding; the floor of an ocean expands outward from a region of growth.

It is fairly well established that new materials are constantly added to the Earth's surface, on the ocean floors, from the upper regions of the mantle. Such materials consist of the lava flow that emerges from cracks in oceanic mountains. As the lava solidifies, a layer of rock is formed, to be followed and pushed away by another layer when the next volcanic eruption occurs.

If we obtain a sample of rock from the region of ocean floor where new floor is seeping out from the guts of our planet, we can determine how long the rock has been there by recording the direction of its magnetic field. This is possible because when lava solidifies it becomes magnetized by the Earth's magnetic field; and this occurs as soon as the lava emerges. Further, it becomes magnetized in a direction corresponding to the direction of the Earth's magnet at that time.

By this technique it has been possible to trace the history of rocks on the ocean floors. It has been found that there is a continuous addition of rocks to the floor, and this causes the floor to grow, or spread.

The technique of rock dating has also shown that the Earth's magnetic field has been reversing its direction at least every 50,000 years. Magnetic field reversals can be traced back 70 million years; more than eighty reversals have occurred in that time. Also, since ocean rocks are quite different from land rocks, it is now assumed that some geographic areas, such as the Red Sea and the Gulf of Aden, may be embryonic oceans. In that same area, the dry land of the Afar Triangle in northern Ethiopia has rocks that are more ocean-like than land-like, implying that this area may be a remnant, a dried ocean.

One might now ask where all the new material goes, once it emerges to the surface of the Earth. It is believed that it eventually returns "to the depths." For example, although the Earth is 4.8 billion years old, the present oceans contain no sediment more than 150 million years old. The original surface of the Earth has then gone somewhere. This indicates that there are currents of materials between the crust and the mantle. We can assume that Pangaea was not the first landmass, but merely the "modern" landmass, the one from which the "modern" continents arose. The events of continental split and drift may have occurred over and over again during the planet's history: a mantle spits out lava, the sea floor spreads, continental plates move; and somewhere, at some time, crust materials are returned to the mantle and things begin again. Over and over the cycle may repeat. It is theory, but it must now be regarded as possible.

When we ponder upon Continental Drift and Sea Floor Spreading, it is obvious that the Earth has not been idle. Changes occur in ocean depths, sizes, and relationships to land. Mountains rise, islands sink, lakes form. Imagine how such massive disruptions can affect the life forms that are developing. Imagine how a flooded cellar affects your household.

Predictions of future changes abound. Some have speculated, not unscientifically, that by 50 million years from now (1) Australia will have moved north, to rub noses with the Eurasian landmass, (2) the eastern portion of Africa will have split off from the mainland, and (3) a section of California will have separated from the continent and drifted northwesterly. By 10 million years from now, Los Angeles will be abreast of San Francisco, and the Mediterranean will have become a dried-up sea that is closed to warships, unless they be amphibious.

Mirror, Mirror: Which Atmosphere Is Best?

It is not only the crust of the Earth that has been changing, and affecting all developing life immeasurably. Our atmosphere has experienced drastic alterations as well.

We are now surrounded by possibly our fourth atmosphere. Our first bonnet occurred when the Earth's mass became large enough and cool enough to attract nearby cosmic gases. This atmosphere lasted until around 400 million years after the birth of the planet.

When the crust cooled further and solidified, a second atmosphere formed, consisting mainly of these gases: ammonia, methane, and water vapor. The water vapor condensed and filled the ocean basins. We were also capped with this atmosphere for about 400 million years. Interestingly, the atmospheres of four of our sister planets—Jupiter, Saturn, Uranus, and Neptune—now contain mostly methane and ammonia gases.

Now, it is believed that the sun's ultraviolet rays decomposed the Earth's methane and ammonia, to release these three products: nitrogen, hydrogen, and carbon. A second source of hydrogen was the water vapor, which split into hydrogen and oxygen. The hydrogen atoms were too light to remain attracted to the Earth, so they escaped. The lonely oxygen atoms then combined with carbon atoms, and presto—carbon dioxide. And presto— our third atmosphere: a nitrogen–carbon dioxide atmosphere. The planet Venus has today a nitrogen–carbon dioxide atmosphere.

The fourth earthly atmosphere evolved because life evolved; plant life. Plants take in carbon dioxide to make their foods, and then release oxygen. This shift, when it first occurred, eventually produced the oxygen which led to our present nitrogen-oxygen atmosphere. Indeed, if all green plants suddenly disappeared tomorrow, most of our atmosphere's oxygen could disappear in 3,000 years.

Gases released by volcanoes have also played a role in the evolution of our atmosphere.

A Hot Time in the Old Town

The Earth's climate has experienced cycles of temperature change. Based on fossil and other evidence, it has been calculated that the average yearly temperature 50 million years ago was around 54° F, whereas now it is around 30° F.

When past temperatures dropped enough to cause massive freezing of some surface waters, there resulted the process called *glaciation,* the formation of glaciers. At least three definite periods of glaciation have occurred: one 400 to 500 million years ago, one 200 to 250 million years ago, and a third ending 10,000 years ago.

The Earth is presently warming, now that it is on its way out of the last glacial age. Since 1920 the average annual temperature of the United States has increased by 3½° F. Even greater increases have occurred in the polar regions; in the Arctic, the average annual temperature has increased by 14° F since 1910.

In some areas, however, there has been evidence of gradual cooling since the 1950s. Whether this shift is only local or temporary, or whether it is the beginning of cooler times, is still uncertain. It is presumed that we can expect another ice age 10 to 15 thousand years from now.

Some interesting highlights of the warming trend are listed below:

(1) One Alaskan glacier retreated two miles in ten years;

(2) In northern Peru, one mountain snow line rose 2,700 feet in sixty years;

(3) In Sweden, a mountain timberline rose sixty-five feet since 1930;

(4) Some trees now encroaching into Alaska, Siberia, and Quebec were never known to exist there before;

(5) Glaciers on the west coast of Greenland have been melting ever since the 1870s.

As animals and plants extend their habitats during a warming trend, they meet new enemies, new competitors for food. Food chains overlap, fights for survival ensue, and those most fit to survive probably do. Many of the rest, whether tree, rabbit, worm, or grass, die.

Other Changes

We may add to the above changes in climate, atmosphere, and land distribution the following: (1) our planet is occasionally exposed to nearby exploding stars, "supernovae," which release intense radiation. There are four recorded sightings of huge balls of fire in the sky, in the years 1006, 1054, 1572, and 1604 A.D. In fact, in our galaxy there occurs, on the average, one supernova explosion every thirty years. But most are probably too remote to affect us significantly. (2) One theory states that the Earth is expanding slowly, and that the moon is retreating slowly from the Earth. The theory is based on the belief that, as the tides roll back and forth on our oceans, they cause a slowing, a braking, action which is reducing the speed of the Earth's spin and allowing it to expand. It is believed that the length of a day increases by 0.002 seconds each 100 years. Presumably, such a loss of Earth spin energy may be transferred to the moon, giving it the momentum needed to move ever farther from the Earth.

By adding all such facts and theories, we reach the summation, to say the very least, that Things change.

How unscientific and unnatural it is then to deny that one species of frog becomes a different species of frog. The evolution of galaxies, stars, a planet's crust, and oceans, in a universe perhaps 15 billion years old, may seem rather remote. But we are right in the middle of Things. If such massive events can occur, think how simple it must be for one kind of green frog to become another kind of green frog.

If centuries of erosion can carve from the Earth the spectacle shown in Figure 5, what marvels might be carved from the tree of life?

Figure 5. Bryce Canyon, Utah, caused by massive erosion.

IV

If I Eat a Cookie, Will It Become Alive?

Should you ask any high school biology student to define "life," he will proceed to list a number of things that a living thing can do. It grows. It moves. It reproduces. Fine.

But there seems to be so much more. You stare at a relative on his deathbed; a "terminal case," says the hospital chart. But you are not staring at a terminal case; nor at one isolated living thing. You are staring at a whole history, a family relationship; love; years of social bondage, of communication, of learning. The terminal case, or the vegetative patient, seems to render any definition of life so impersonal, so mechanical, so remote.

Or you glance shyly at a pregnant woman's belly. Two lives. One of them going through an unbelievably complicated development, yet a development repeated billions of times with but few errors. How can one define life mechanically here? Quickening? Birth? Crying? Who knows.

Or the yeast tablet on that shelf. Drop it in water and swisssh—you suddenly get millions of living and active yeast cells previously dormant. Or a radish seed is casually dropped into a child's garden; a few days later: a dormant radish seed becomes a living and growing plant. Or the "dead," frozen goldfish revived and swimming. Or frozen human sperm suddenly revived and able to fertilize and help form a person; a living person.

Yes, it is difficult to define life. But whatever it is, it is not a Thing, but an Activity; a Process. A living thing may be a Thing, but its life is an Activity.

When we come down to the simplest forms of living things, we find that it becomes more and more difficult for us to decide if they are alive or not; if they are "living" or "chemical." Science decides, but only arbitrarily.

It appears that "life" is but a convenient term used to designate a particular degree of organization of chemicals; a particular complexity. At least this is the way we must look at it when we look at its evolution. When we observe the actions of a terminal patient we are searching for different things than when we observe the actions of humanity, of the human species as a whole. To ask what a person is, is quite different from asking what humanity is.

The greater the organization and the complexity, the more a living thing can do on its own; the more obvious is its "life" to us. We would not hesitate to differentiate between a man and a stone, even if the latter is occasionally used to describe the former. But we might hesitate in defining a virus as being alive, even if it does perform some activities that are also performed by higher, truly living, organisms.

Another point of importance is the following: The chemicals found in a dog could not do "dog activities" if not *organized* into a dog. This shows then that life does not merely reflect a number of chemical substances, but it reflects how these substances are arranged and what they can do when they are so arranged.

Many of the foods we eat are not alive, usually. But do they become alive after we eat them? No. In fact, "they" no longer exist as such. That cookie becomes disorganized by our gut; its basic elements get into the bloodstream, and eventually reach some cells. In the cells, these chemicals are reorganized into a "you," or a "me," and no longer into a "cookie." So the cookie does not become alive; instead, its chemicals become reorganized and incorporated into a living machine.

There is another problem in the attempt to define life. It appears that there are degrees of life, and we must specify which degree, which level, we mean.

Look at a human being. He displays five levels of life: (1) *Cell life*—my liver cells are alive, but they cannot do much by themselves; (2) *Organ life*—my liver cells, when organized into a liver, can do things that one liver cell alone cannot do; (3) *Organismal life*—my liver, when in the same body as my gut, my kidneys, and assorted other organs, can perform even better and more extensively, since what it does depends largely on what my other organs are doing; (4) *Vegetative life*—even if I am unconscious, I can still breathe, and my liver and kidneys still function, since a portion of my brain maintains some body coordination, even if I am unaware of it; and finally, (5) *Psychic life*—my conscious brain displays another degree of life; it is often the first to die, as in the vegetative patient; and it is apparently the last level of life to become established in the developing embryo.

Because of the above intricacies and complexities, we must be very careful of how we define life. One cannot assign the "life" tag to anything merely because it displays a certain complexity. At least a second criterion is needed, besides complexity; that is *self-initiation,* already mentioned in terms of ameba activity. A living thing can cause itself to do things. It cannot cause itself to evolve; but once it has been evolved, it can cause itself to respond to its environment in order to survive.

We might say therefore that there is such a thing as a biological *Triangle of Causation,* in higher animals at least. Three causative agents tell you what to do. One of them is yourself. Let me explain.

The first agent is heredity, the first to be used before your birth and shortly thereafter; the second is environment, gradually affecting your heredity more and more; and thirdly, there develops a self, a "you," as you age and become more and more able to alter and plan your environment, and to suppress at least some of your heredity. Thus, Heredity + Environment + Self = You, the reader, today.

Life: What Are the Odds?

It must be obvious then that one should have the greatest enthusiasm for an evolutionary process that has yielded the processes of life and of human life. But by now it must also be obvious that the odds are poor indeed for life to evolve, for this complex of activities to become possible.

Needed are the proper atmosphere, the proper chemicals, the proper temperature, the proper level of radiation —all of which at extremes can prevent life from arising. For example, if our Earth's orbit were a bare 10 percent nearer the sun than it is now, life could exist on only 20 percent of this planet. As it is, life exists nearly everywhere on the globe.

Yes, the odds are small. But obviously, not impossible.

Even now, perhaps 15 billion years after the Big Bang, 99 percent of all the material stuff of our universe is still in the extreme simple stages of hydrogen and helium gases, the two simplest, the least complicated, of the 105 elements which we know. In fact it seems that the universe is much more often *dis*organizing than organizing. Disorder seems more common than evolution.

But if certain sites of the universe temporarily trap enough energy, then evolution can occur, and the complexities of life as described earlier can arise. That is obviously what has happened on our Earth, near a charitable sun providing energy for simple chemicals to evolve to become organized into plants. By then storing this solar energy, plant cells produce foods which become in part the fuels of life for hungry animals.

Fortunate indeed is man to be here, in view of such odds against his arrival.

V

Some Gears in the System

As a final note in our brief survey of universal and earthly change, and of life activity, let us try to establish some standards; some rules by which nature seems to play the evolution game. This approach will, it is hoped, bring evolution in focus in terms of daily and downtown life activity.

If you scrutinize carefully the development of a human society, or a baseball team, or a factory, or a human baby, or a universe, you might find that evolution seems to follow the same general trend at all levels of complexity. Figure 6 illustrates the apparent trend followed by anything that evolves. In the figure, five steps are listed, and defined below:

(1) *Uniformity*—all parts are pretty much alike. For example, most kids on an elementary school baseball team can play all the positions on the field; most men in a primitive society were hunters or farmers; most production lines in a new factory produce the same thing; most

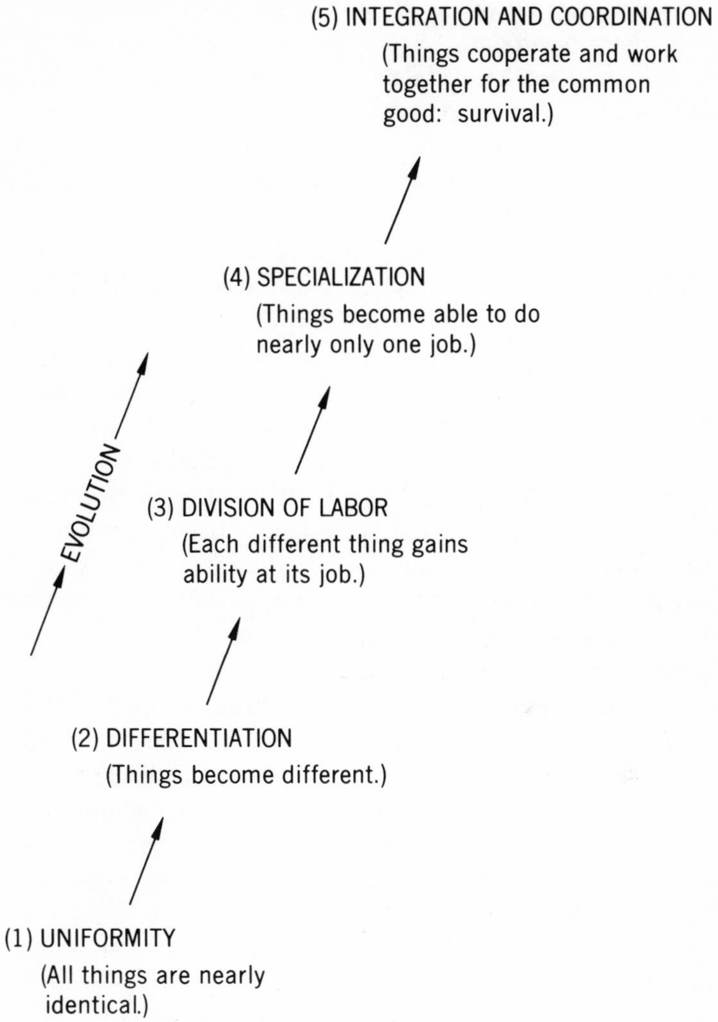

(5) INTEGRATION AND COORDINATION
(Things cooperate and work
together for the common
good: survival.)

(4) SPECIALIZATION
(Things become able to do
nearly only one job.)

EVOLUTION

(3) DIVISION OF LABOR
(Each different thing gains
ability at its job.)

(2) DIFFERENTIATION
(Things become different.)

(1) UNIFORMITY
(All things are nearly
identical.)

Figure 6. Outline of general stages of evolution.

cells of an early human embryo look alike; most atoms
in the universe are either hydrogen or helium.

(2) *Differentiation*—as the evolutionary process continues, things become different from each other. As a result, there occurs a . . .

(3) . . . *Division of labor*—some kids resort to pitching only, while others stick to first base. Some farmers become blacksmiths, others bankers, bakers, tradesmen, or leaders. The factory diversifies. The human embryo acquires muscles, bones, blood, etc.

(4) *Specialization*—after a while, the different components learn to do their jobs more and more efficiently. The pitcher becomes a terrible batter; the engineer never sees a cow; it would cost millions to alter a specialized production line in a factory; and my muscles can do nothing but muscle work, my heart can only pump blood, my eyes cannot taste, and my ears cannot see.

(5) *Integration and Coordination*—if evolution continues, the evolving components finally become more and more efficiently organized by some central agency, and become more and more firmly integrated. The central agency may be a government, a national baseball league, a labor union, a body's brain, etc.

Incidentally, although the last stages—specialization, integration, and coordination—are evolutionarily ideal, they are quite precarious as well. Overspecialization in a fixed and rigid society, for example, can be maintained indefinitely but only if the environment remains steady. If anything out of the ordinary comes along, poof—the whole system can fall.

If professional baseball were to eliminate the shortstop position, the professional shortstop might have to quit baseball. If schools dropped history courses from their curriculum, history teachers might have to sell hotdogs. If people ever have no further need for razor blades, the electric shaver companies might triple their income, but

Gillette might get scrapped. If the brain suffers a stroke, the patient may become a "vegetable."

Sidelights of an Evolving Thing

It should be obvious by now that Things do seem to follow some standard evolutionary laws, if they do manage to evolve.

But while the process of evolution is leading Things to greater integration and coordination, other major developments take place as well. These do not appear at any one step in Figure 6, but can be observed at all steps, gradually improving in efficiency.

(1) *Feedback.* Ideally all components of an evolving Thing are interconnected. Take a town for example: if the baker in the town produces too many doughnuts on Tuesday and people do not buy all of them, he learns to bake fewer doughnuts on Wednesday. This is called "feedback control" because some information was "fed back" to the baker, and this information helped to determine what he would do next.

For another example, if your human brain tells your human hand to pick up a pencil, your hand will feed back to the brain information saying that it has done so. Again, if a congressional action on Thursday is unpopular, pickets may abound on Friday.

As a society, or an animal body, or any Thing evolves, there arises an increased ability to feed back information from one part, or member, to another.

(2) *Adaptation.* Under constant stress to change, if a Thing evolves it does so because it did change; it did adapt. But it must be stressed that no Thing adapts on its own. It is Mother Nature that usually causes Things to

evolve; at least this was true before the arrival of Human Nature. No animal or plant can tell itself that it wishes to adapt; if it adapts, it was purely a matter of chance. The process of adaptation, and of the resulting evolution of species, will be discussed in Chapters V to XI.

(3) *Polarization.* Even as a Thing, say a human society, evolves, its members tend to separate in some ways. In fact, it appears that if this does not occur, the Thing will not evolve, but its parts will remain uniform.

For example, some slight shift in your opinion about an issue on which you were undecided can result from something you see, hear, or read. Even after years of indecision, one word can cause you to polarize towards one view or the other, can make you a solid advocate, or a solid opponent. Any slight shift to one side or another in the evolution of a galaxy, of a society, or a baseball team, yields greater differences. If teams A and B are equally proficient except for one batter on team A who bats just slightly better than all others on both teams, by the end of the season of play team A might be far ahead of team B in final standings.

In fact, without polarization there could not occur differentiation and division of labor. To create another example: Joe and Sam both own grocery stores. Joe manages to sell one, and only one, item cheaper than Sam does; all other items are equally priced in both stores. People then begin to buy from Joe more than from Sam. Joe can now afford to cut other prices. As a result, he soon owns a chain of supermarkets, while Sam sells hotdogs.

Polarization, whether political, sociological, or biological, seems to be a necessary ingredient of the evolutionary process. If two groups of fishes are exactly alike, except for the presence in one of a lung-like structure, and if it ever happens that the waters begin to evaporate and the fishes are in trouble, then the fishes with "lungs" live and the others die. A slight difference yielding all the difference in the world. Indeed this was the case in the evolution of fishes to amphibians, as we will see.

(4) *Socialization.* If Things evolve, they gradually achieve a complexity at which the evolving parts become more and more interrelated and, beyond that, interdependent as well. These two phenomena, interrelation and interdependence, surely define a society; the human society, the bee or ant society, or a society of forest plants.

But what about a "society" of engineered matter? Well, picture the complex of global computer networks that can track an orbiting spacecraft.

MOTHER NATURE: JUDGE AND JURY

VI

To Fit In:
That's the Key to Success

Facts. They very often provide us with security. When you find yourself entwined in a discussion, your face may reflect the strain to remember the statistic, the date, or the name that you read the evening before. Facts provide foundation and credibility to your arguments.

This applies equally to the biologist. As he scans the world of life, he can drain countless facts from it, and this creates an enormous enthusiasm in him. He may then boldly look you in the eye and call his *theory* of evolution a *law* of evolution; a "fact of nature." Whether his enthusiasm is misplaced or not remains inconsequential to this chapter. What I wish to survey here is a set of facts that sprinkle the horizon of our present biosphere. What do we see today that gives us an indication that an evolution might have occurred?

The Tailored Suit

If you have ever joined a new community, a new club, or a new school, you may have found it difficult to adapt at first. You may have found that your previous habits or attitudes were not suited to the new situation. And the only way you could "fit in" was to change, or at least to pretend to do so. This was a "psychic," or a "social," adaptation.

Similarly, but in a different manner, other living things besides human beings must adapt to their environment if they are to remain in it. One of the most intriguing phenomena of nature is that organisms *are* so well adapted to their way of life and to their environment. Another intriguing phenomenon—perhaps the most intriguing of all—is that not only are organisms well adapted to their environment, but they can *become* adapted to a new environment.

Before we recall some examples of adaptations that you may have observed, let us review three generalities of nature.

It is usually the case that nature prevents two different species of animals or of plants from occupying the same niche—a niche can be defined as the role which an organism plays in the web of life. For example, if two different animal species were to restrict their diet to the very same food, in time and place, then one species would almost always outcompete the other, not unlike two fine ladies who notice that they are wearing identical gowns.

Another natural phenomenon is this: if the environment of a species changes, and if the change requires a different mode of life, then either the species changes as well, or it dies out.

Let us then remember these two realities of life as

we proceed: competition (for food, space, mates) and the occasional need to adapt. The two are closely linked. If, for example, a gradual change in climate, the formation of an island, the drying of a lake, or a forest fire should force two different species to seek a new source of food, the less competent species must find a source other than its competitor's, or it will die. Thus, to survive in such a circumstance, the two disturbed species must adapt; and competition between the two promotes *different* adaptations.

A third natural reality may present itself. If a species becomes so highly specialized that it is totally dependent on a certain type of environment, or on one source of food, then any local change will often cause the destruction of that species.

For example, the dependence of the koala, the Australian "teddy bear," on eucalyptus leaves is ideal for that animal, as long as eucalyptus leaves are available.

The perilous irony of overspecialization was placed in evolutionary focus in Chapter V.

Adaptation to a Food Source

You have probably heard of Charles Darwin. He was a very deliberate and scientific man; in one study he performed an extensive analysis of the beaks of the many kinds of finches seen on the Galápagos Islands. Finches belong to the same family of birds as the canary, the cardinal, and the sparrows. They all possess stout beaks adapted to crush seeds, the main item in their diet. But the beaks of different finches, Darwin found, are strikingly adapted either to grasp, probe, or crush, depending on the bird's preferred type of seed.

Moreover, the different beaks of certain other finches

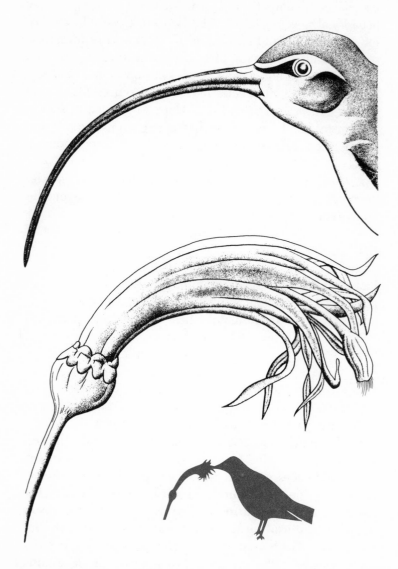

Figure 7. Beak of Hemignathus obscurus (upper). Flower of a lobelia, that provides part of the diet of the bird.

are used to probe flowers, eat fruit, search tree barks for insects, or bore into wood. One type of finch is even able to grasp a stick in its beak and use it as a tool to probe out insects from trees. Thus, different species of finches can all live together quite peacefully, as long as each sticks to its own diet.

Another fascinating example, in other kinds of birds, is a long curved beak able to reach into the depths of the long curved flowers which provide a source of nectar. The bird shown in Figure 7 uses its beak mainly to probe tree barks for insects; but it also uses it to obtain nectar from the curved flowers of a lobelia, shown in Figure 7. Notice the correspondence in curvature.

Adaptation to an Environment

Most plants are either land plants or aquatic plants. The former usually die if submerged in water, and the latter likewise fare poorly if removed from their normal habitat. Some plants, however, are not so specialized, but are truly amphibious. For example, the water marigold shown in Figure 8 has two kinds of leaves: one kind adapted to water, the other to the air above the water. Notice that the leaves above water are solid, and not cut into tiny "threads." Each kind of leaf is an adaptation to its environment.

Similar leaf adaptations are found in several other aquatic plants. In some, the same plant can be made to grow different kinds of leaves merely by exposing the plant to air or to water. The arrowleaf, shown in Figure 9, produces a thin, buoyed leaf when in water, and a broad, stronger leaf when on land. The same part of the stem can yield either leaf, depending on the environment. In addition, the leaves in water lack the protective *cuticle*

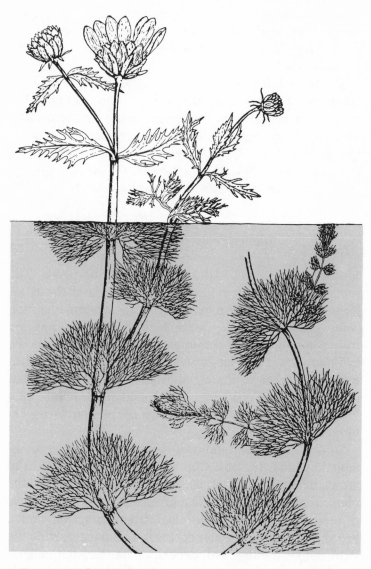

Figure 8. Submerged and emersed portions of water marigold.

Figure 9. The arrow leaf grown on land, partially submerged, and grown completely in water.

covering found in surfaced leaves; a cuticle would prevent the absorption of nutrients directly from the water, whereas surfaced leaves have no need to absorb, since they receive their nutrients through the roots. The cuticle also prevents the drying of surfaced leaves.

Animals also display innumerable adaptations to their environment. Some forms mimic others; some butterfly species bear a striking resemblance to other butterfly species that are unpalatable to birds. This serves to preserve the more palatable mimic from a "birdfood fate."

Many animals are truly camouflaged into their environment, and this clearly offers an advantage. Figure 10 shows an example of such camouflage among insects, a group most adept at such trickery.

Some animals display very striking "lures" to attract prey. If you can stand it, glance quickly at the angler fish in Figure 11. It has a worm-like structure at the end of a "stick," which it uses as bait to attract other fish. The

Figure 10. *Biston betularia* L., the Peppered Moth and its black form *carbonaria*, at rest on soot-covered Oak trunk near Birmingham.

Figure 11. Angler fish luring smaller fish by dummy bait.

"worm" and the "stick" are really a part of the angler fish.

Also, the flowers of some species of orchids resemble female bees and attract, of course, male bees. The latter then unknowingly pollinate the flowers. This adaptation is a means to ensure the pollination so crucial to the continuation of the orchid species. (See Figure 12.)

Some animals even have more than one set of certain structures; they use the one that suits a particular environment. If the environment changes, they merely shift to

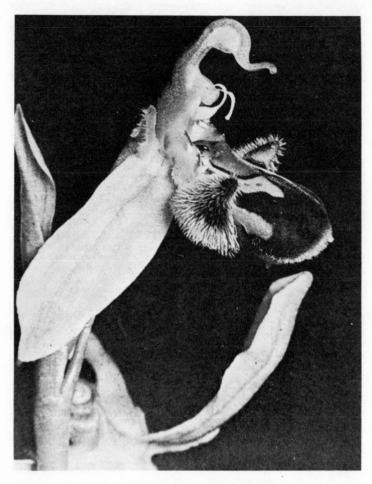

Figure 12. Orchid flower resembling female bee.

the spare parts. The lungfish, for example, can breathe in two ways: in clear water it uses its gills; but in foul or stagnant water low in oxygen, it rises to the surface to gulp in air, much as we do with our lungs. There are presently six species of lungfish in the world. A similar group of fish, the "walking catfish," have begun to frighten little children and dogs, as they roam across Florida highways for jaunts of one-fourth mile or more. The rear parts of their gills have a lung-like structure which enables them to breathe outside the water. The fish also have, on some fins, a spine that strengthens the fin enough to be used as a limb to creep along the ground.

Perhaps the most fascinating example of adaptation is how an embryo develops to become able to fit into the world when it is born. Here also is an example of the general process of evolution as outlined in Figure 6, from identical cells, to cells more and more different, and so on. Figure 13 shows five early stages in embryonic develop-

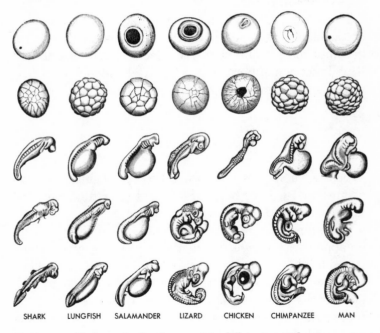

SHARK   LUNGFISH   SALAMANDER   LIZARD   CHICKEN   CHIMPANZEE   MAN

Figure 13. Embryonic development in different vertebrate species.

SHARK   LUNGFISH   SALAMANDER   LIZARD   CHICKEN   CHIMPANZEE   MAN

Figure 14. Later stages of development in species shown in Figure 13.

ment in seven different species of animals—lizard, chimpanzee, lungfish, man, shark, chicken, and salamander. Can you identify them?

If you cannot, then turn to Figure 14 for two later stages of development in each of the seven species, as each becomes more adapted to the specific environment that it will face when born. The left-to-right sequence in Figure 14 is the same as in Figure 13.

Leftovers

Whenever a species is well adapted to a habitat, we can assume that it is its body organs and their functions that are well adapted.

Therefore, we may wonder why many animals are equipped with organs or other structures for which there is absolutely no use. We must be cautious, however, when asserting that an organ serves no purpose. It could well be that the purpose has not yet been discovered. But in some cases, the evidence for "uselessness" is overwhelming. If all members of a species have something they are not using, we can then assume that it must be a "souvenir" of the past; it must be a leftover from times when that species, or its ancestor, did use it.

Such structures, as well as functions or behaviors, are said to be "vestigial."

Examples in man include his pointed canine teeth, his body hair, ear muscles, and muscles in the skin. The horse's skin can twitch easily, but ours cannot although it still bears unused muscles.

And everyone knows about the appendix. In plant-eating mammals such as the rabbit there is a large pouch, nearly eighteen inches long, that branches off from the intestines. In this pouch some plant constituents are digested. In man, where that large pouch should be there is only a short, obviously useless and degenerate appendix.

To list other examples of vestigial organs: (1) the whale has no hindlimbs, yet there are small useless bones in the positions where the hindlimbs would exit from the body; (2) some snakes have the same useless bones in the same places; and (3) the New Zealand kiwi bird, although flightless, has rudimentary wing structures that it never uses.

It is not only in adults that one sees adaptations left over from the past. Take the human embryo, for example. At some stages of its early development it has some features strikingly reminiscent of other backboned animals. It has a tail, which at six weeks of pregnancy is one-sixth of the total body length; then it shortens. (See Figure 13.) Although it happens very rarely, some babies are born with a tail that did not regress, but that remains to lengths of as much as eight inches.

Another example from the human embryo is seen in the structures reminiscent of a fish. When a baby fish forms, five outside indentations appear on each side of its body, behind the head region. Meanwhile, five sets of indentations form inside its "throat." The outside and the inside indentations meet and pierce, resulting in ten openings that then become lined with gills. In the forming human baby, both sets of indentations, outside and inside, form, but then never pierce. They later smooth out and disappear. However, in rare cases one pair may pierce through, and the person is born with a hole in his neck, to one side of his windpipe.

There are many other examples in the newborn of features abnormally left over from other animals. Sometimes babies do not lose some structures which they should have lost, such as the human baby born with webbed feet or hands, or with more than one set of nipples, as in cats and mice.

Retention of a Harmful Trait

As stated earlier, if two species compete, the species more fit for the environment will usually win. The same is true of competition between the members of one species. In these ways are the useless or harmful traits eventually lost, and replaced by more adaptable and useful traits.

Therefore, it may be surprising to see the persistence in some parts of our globe of sickle-cell anemia, a fatal blood cell disease of human beings.

The reason for the persistence of this disease, however, is that some of those who suffer a mild form of it also have a resistance to malaria.

Here is a situation where two harmful traits are paired off against each other: sickle-cell anemia, and susceptibility to malaria. One disease becomes a possible "preventative" against the other. If you think about it, this means that in malaria-prone nations many people with sickle-cell anemia can often reach reproductive age, even if they contract malaria in infancy.

"Adaptation" in this case can occur more easily if a harmful trait is kept. This is contrary to all that has been discussed in this chapter.

For the purpose of subsequent discussions, let us now elaborate upon the hereditary basis of the sickle cell-to-malaria relationship mentioned above.

Except for your sex cells, all of the cells in you—liver or bone or skin or heart cells—are *somatic* cells. Each somatic cell has, in its nucleus, at least one pair of genes for each and every trait that you have inherited. Of any one pair of genes in any individual, one of the genes may be *dominant* and the other *recessive*. What this means is that the dominant gene prevents the expression of its partner, the recessive. Therefore there are three possible combinations of the two genes: (1) there may be one dominant and one recessive, (2) both genes may be of the dominant kind, or (3) both may be recessive.

To make things simpler than they are in actuality, let us apply the above to the trait called "the color of your eyes." If you have blue eyes, each cell in your eye's iris has two genes which cause the formation of blue pigments. All other cells in your body also have the "eye-color" genes, but they are therein "turned off," for they are not functional in other cells. What would a liver cell do with eye-color genes?

If you have brown eyes, however, each iris cell has two genes that cause the formation of brown pigments. But a person may have brown eyes, yet have one of each gene, a brown-eye gene, B, and a blue-eye gene, b. This implies that the brown-eye gene is dominant to the other.

A mixture of a dominant gene and a recessive gene in a person's cells is called a *heterozygous* condition. Two brown-eye, or two blue-eye genes constitute *homozygous* conditions.

Notice the three possibilities in Figure 15-A. You should

	(A) TRAIT: EYE COLOR	
B B	Cell from iris of brown-eyed person. Within the cell, only 2 of the many genes are shown: those 2 assumed responsible for eye color. Instead of drawing the genes, they are represented by letters.	This person is HOMOZYGOUS DOMINANT for eye color. He has brown eyes.
B b	Cell from iris of brown-eyed person.	This person is HETEROZYGOUS for eye color. Since there is present a "B" gene, it will mask the "b" gene, and the eyes will be brown, not blue.
b b	Cell from iris of blue-eyed person.	This person is HOMOZYGOUS RECESSIVE for eye color. He has blue eyes.

	(B) TRAIT: SICKLE-CELL ANEMIA	
S S	Cell from blood of person destined to die of sickle-cell anemia, a condition in which the red blood cells cannot carry enough oxygen to feed the person's tissues well.	This person is HOMOZYGOUS DOMINANT for sickle-cell anemia, and has the disease.
S s	Cell from blood of person not slated to die of the disease. Contrary to eye color, this trait occurs, in its violent form, only when homozygous dominant.	This person is HETEROZYGOUS, and has a milder form of the disease. Coincidentally he is less able to provide shelter for the organism that causes malaria.
s s	Cell from blood of person not affected at all by the disease.	This person is HOMOZYGOUS RECESSIVE for the trait, hence has neither the dominant (lethal) form, nor the heterozygous (mild) form.

now read the descriptions in this figure before proceeding. (Page 60.)

Now, every person displays thousands of traits besides eye color; hence the presence of thousands and thousands of genes in each cell. One other trait is sickle-cell anemia. This can be fatal when both genes for the trait are present in a person's cells; i.e., when a person is in the homozygous condition for the gene responsible, gene S. Thus, fatal sickle-cell anemia usually occurs in the SS condition. But when heterozygous, Ss, there results only a milder form of the disease.

This heterozygous condition is the one that is malaria-resistant. Now, since having one S gene does help some people, the gene remains in the population, even if this means that it will occasionally occur in the homozygous, fatal condition, SS. The gene is not lost from the population, as most other harmful genes would be.

As it turns out then, the Ss person has a greater chance of surviving in malaria-prone areas than either the SS or ss person: the SS person will probably die of sickle-cell anemia, and the ss person stands a 25 percent less chance of reaching adulthood than does the Ss individual because he will probably contract malaria.

The phenomenon is described further in Figure 15-B.

Now, it is also important to know *why* the Ss combination offers resistance to malaria. Simply, the person is resistant because he does have some abnormality, although mild, of his blood cells; the abnormality is just adequate to refuse to offer shelter for the one-celled organism that causes malaria.

Figure 15A. Description of three possible gene combinations for eye color.
Figure 15B. The three possible gene combinations for sickle-cell anemia.

A condition such as this, in which a heterozygous mixture of genes offers an advantage, is referred to as *hybrid vigor*. It is often hybrid vigor that permits the retention of a harmful gene in a population. We have analyzed only one trait subjected to hybrid vigor; there are many more.

Figure 16 consolidates several of the concepts and processes defined in the present section. It is shown that sex cells have only one gene of each pair; this is necessary since fertilization, by which two sex cells fuse, results in a cell that again will have the two genes of each pair. If a sperm and an egg each had both genes, then the new baby would end up with four of the genes for a trait; this could be fatal.

Complacency

Now that we have surveyed examples of organisms that adapt to food sources and to environmental conditions, examples of structures not utilized, and an example of the retention of a harmful gene, we may think that all forms of life are constantly adapting. It is more probable, however, that adaptation is a temporary, occasional phenomenon.

For example, one would expect that natural selection would "leave alone" any species of plant or animal that is able to survive a wide range of environmental changes. If a tree can survive in a wide range of temperatures, a change in temperature will not affect it as it would a tree that can survive in only a narrow range.

A second reason why a species might remain relatively unchanged for a long time could be a lack of appreciable environmental change. If a species is well adapted to an environment, and that environment is stable, then the species could survive indefinitely.

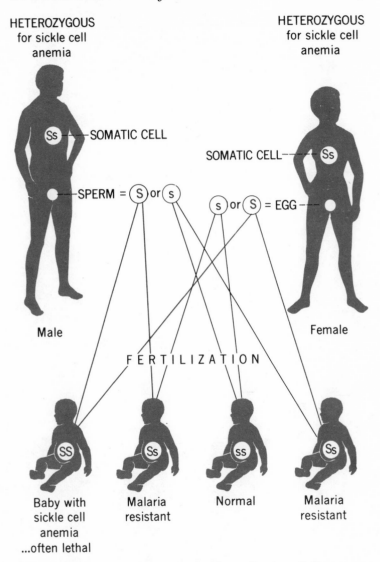

Figure 16. The couple above can produce offspring of three types: SS, Ss, or ss. If a heterozygous condition permits "hybrid vigor," as it permits malaria resistance in this example, a gene tends to remain in the population, even if it is lethal when homozygous.

It is perhaps the time to begin wondering how mankind would fare if his environment changes too rapidly, or if it changes slowly but with results beyond the range to which man has adapted.

VII

Look Over There.
See the Evolution?

Whenever competition arises between animals as a result of newly imposed climate or soil conditions, or because of any other factor that favors the survival of one trait over another, we call the process Natural Selection.

But just what is it? Who is "Mother Nature"? And how does she "select"?

Very simply, Mother Nature is everything around us and in us. Mother Nature is a hungry fox, a windstorm, an empty stomach, a huge human footstep about to destroy the architecture of an ant hill, or a huge meteor about to destroy the Earth. In the analogy of Joe and Sam and their markets, Mother Nature is the consumer who selects Joe's prices in preference to Sam's. In the case of the orchid that looks like a female bee, Mother Nature is the male bee that selects that flower in preference to another. In the case of the persistence of hybrid vigor in sickle-cell anemia, Mother Nature consists of the defective blood cells that deny an adequate shelter to malaria organisms.

Most often, the Mother Nature that performs Natural Selection consists of many factors, all of which have a say in the final outcome of a trait; whether it will persist, or be lost in the shuffle of generations.

To see and record a living thing as it actually changes some of its traits at the hands of Mother Nature is highly satisfying to the evolutionist. Let us survey some actual observations of "change," either seen in nature or induced in a laboratory.

Artificial Selection? Or Is It?

As early as 1937, scientists found that it took very little time for a favorable trait to overcome an abnormal and unfavorable one. By starting with 4,000 abnormal fruit flies in a cage, then adding a few normal ones, competition was artificially established. By 235 days later, after many generations (it takes only about fourteen days for fruit flies to mature), the percent of abnormal flies had dropped from nearly 100 percent to 28 percent; by 436 days, 99 percent of the flies were of the normal type.

Clearly, a selection process had allowed the normal offspring to survive more often than the abnormal ones. It could be argued that this was a natural selection compelled to operate under artificial conditions. It might be erroneous to call the selection that occurred an artificial selection; scientists did not select, but merely encaged the flies so as to have a front-row seat as natural selection did its work.

Another study used fruit flies with a harmful gene that caused many of them to die young, and others to develop more slowly than is normal. The stock of flies was raised, generation after generation, until by the tenth generation their viability, the ability to survive, improved markedly. By the fiftieth generation the flies were almost normal, including their development time. The investigators thus had observed, by recording 410,784 flies, the "weeding out" of unfavorable traits by natural selection. The abnormal "baby" flies often died and could not pass on their genes as often as the normal "babies" could.

The same phenomenon was observed in the red checker moth. By artificial selection—human selection—British scientists were able to obtain a pure strain of a moth with an abnormal wing color; this could have been disastrous to the moth. Assured of little or no crossbreeding between this type and the normal type in nature, the scientists released the little Frankenstein moths, and within a brief span of five years the descendants of the abnormal strain had shifted to a population with normal wing coloration!

Some British geneticists spent twenty-four years studying the change in a rather peculiar trait in the scarlet tiger moth. Some of the moths have two spots on each wing, others have many. The number of spots is an inherited trait. There was found to be a gradual decline in the percent of two-spot moths from 11 percent of the moth population in 1940 to 2 percent in 1961, this time with no human intervention.

There is also the classical example of the recent rapid change in coloration of moths inhabiting tree trunks in England and nearby areas. There are two types, one with light gray or white wings, and one with black wings and a black body. The black color is believed due to a mutation. Clearly, the light color would be selected in preference to the dark color if the moth inhabits a light background, which it did until the industrial revolution. Return to Figure 10 to see the dark moth camouflaged against a tree bark—if you can find the moth.

Since the black form of the moth was first discovered in 1848, there had been seen a gradual increase in black moths. By 1895, 98 percent of the species was black. Further, this rapid change occurred almost solely in urban manufacturing districts. As tree trunks darkened, and as the lichen thereon died, dark coloration became advantageous to hide from birds. Several experiments have been performed to verify that natural selection—in this case, hungry birds—selects in favor of the color most suited to the environment, and selects against the other color. On light trunks, the dark moth population decreases, and on dark trunks the light moth population decreases.

Often, even if nature selects against a trait, for some reason the inferior trait may remain in the population in small, but persisting, numbers. We have already seen this to be the case for sickle-cell anemia. This was also shown in fruit flies in a study similar to the 1937 experiment described earlier, but this time with a different abnormality. As for the first study, by 235 days the prevalence of the trait again dropped from 100 percent to 28 percent. However, it then dropped to 15 percent and stabilized there. It would not drop any further. Even if it was obvious that nature selected against the trait, about 15 out of every 100 newborn fruit flies displayed the recessive trait, generation after generation.

Now, since the trait was recessive, that means that the only flies that could display it were those homozygous for the recessive gene. That 15 flies out of each 100 displayed the destructive trait was an indication that there were many more than 15 that were harboring the recessive gene. In other words, there must have been many of the "normal" flies, the 85 percent, that were heterozygous for the trait because it provided them with hybrid vigor to combat something else.

A 1948 study with fruit flies that were made semisterile showed that by two months after the start of an experiment, natural selection had completed its task. Most of the semisterility was eliminated from the fly population. But again there were always new cases appearing—another example of hybrid vigor. There are probably many such examples in the human species, examples yet undiscovered.

Reviewing Figure 16, remember that the heterozygotes are selected more often than homozygote normals, and of course, more often than the homozygote abnormals. This situation results: an inferior gene remains in the population, occasionally to appear as a homozygous abnormal condition. The gene could be the dominant gene of a pair, or it could be the recessive one, depending on the trait.

Such is the kind of factual evidence that demonstrates to scientists that new variations arise constantly in animals and in plants. In fact, geneticists face a constant struggle to *prevent* change, as in domesticated plants. Also, since 1909 when the first white-eyed fruit fly was discovered (normal eye color is red), more than 5,000 mutants have been found—with all sorts of differences—among the more than 20 million fruit flies examined since that time.

Gene mutations are now known for every kind of plant or animal that has been subjected to genetic study—corn, snapdragons, coffee, cacao, mice, molds, bacteria, man, and so on. Further, mutation rates (how often any one kind of gene mutates in a population) can be determined and can be altered experimentally by x rays, ultraviolet light, temperature changes, and a variety of chemicals.

A Leash on Life

Long before man learned the laws of genetics, he was able to breed some animals and plants to acquire traits he desired. He domesticated the dog perhaps as early as 9000 B.C., and the cat and goat around 7000 B.C. Domesticated cattle and pigs came later.

It is assumed possible to determine if fossilized bones belonged to domesticated animals, or to their wild contemporaries. There are obvious structural differences in their respective bones. Studying 8,000-year-old sheep bones from Turkey, paleontologists found structural differences by using specialized techniques. For example, the alignment of crystals within the bone material differs markedly. Bone tissues also appear different under the microscope. Although such evidence is still fragmentary, there may be some justification for the correlation of bone structure to the duties of domesticated animals.

If offspring result when man breeds two different species of plants or animals together, they are called *hybrids*. Used in this way, the term is not related to its usage in "hybrid vigor."

Hybrids may be sterile, or they may be able to breed together or with the original parents to produce offspring.

This form of adaptation is obviously not due to natural selection, but to artificial selection. Man's goal is usually to produce hybrids that will then continue to produce offspring like themselves, and not like the original parents. This is how a "true line" can be created artificially.

Let us review some examples of artificially adapted species.

(1) Corn, which has been cultivated for 5,000 years, was hybridized with the intention of producing high-yield crops, and crops that were highly resistant to disease. The

corn plant thus formed is not able to reproduce itself, but is completely dependent on man to disperse its seeds. The farmer must reseed his fields every year.

(2) In October of 1970, the Nobel Prize for Peace was awarded for the development of high-yielding varieties of Mexican wheats. These new forms grow well over a wide range of soils on the Earth—a new feat in cereal breeding. Using the artificially adapted hybrids, farmers in West Pakistan have nearly doubled cereal production in the brief span of five years. India's wheat crop increased from 12 million tons to 21 million tons in the same span of time. This shows the life-or-death advantage that can be derived from proper hybridization to produce better plants.

It should be noted, however, that even when a true line is established, mutations continually cause complications. Wheat, for example, is often susceptible to a "stem rust disease"; and the organism that causes the disease is constantly mutating. Hence, plant breeders must continually compete with the disease by creating new and more resistant hybrids of wheat. The seeds of new types of wheats are stored, for example, at the National Seed Storage Laboratory at Fort Collins, Colorado. As of May 1967, there were stored for safekeeping seeds of 400 different kinds of mutants of oats, 112 different kinds of tomatoes, 310 barley lines, and 110 red pericarp lines of corn.

(3) Oranges (selected for being sweet, juicy, thin-skinned, and almost seedless), bananas (selected for resistance to diseases such as the fungus called "Panama disease"), dogs (with now over 100 varieties), poultry (selected for more white meat, etc.), forest trees, silk-worm, tobacco, cattle, pigs, and so on—the list is nearly endless. And the means of breeding are increasing rapidly. For example, it is now possible to freeze ram, bull, and

stallion semen in pellet forms, for transportation around the world. We can even preserve bull and buffalo semen at room temperature in a solution of coconut water; the semen can then be used for artificial insemination up to four days after collection to increase animal protein supplies for developing nations.

It becomes obvious not only that constant adaptation does occur now, but that man is in a constant struggle to prevent change in the organisms he has hybridized for his purposes.

Resistance: To Drug a "Bug"

Whenever some organisms adapt to an environment that was created by man, if that environment was designed purposely to destroy them we say that they have become "resistant" to it.

A few examples will further illustrate the fact of adaptation as witnessed by the biologist in recent years.

There was a time when penicillin was used for nearly every conceivable type of infection. Then, suddenly, physicians began to notice a sharp decline in its potency. Subsequently, new antibiotics were developed and used, and periodically these produced the same outcome.

What happened? Why did a species of bacteria once susceptible to a drug suddenly become immune to it? Suffice it to repeat that all living things are apparently subject to spontaneous and continual changes in the hereditary material of their cells. Such mutations may enable an organism to do something it could not do before. Or a mutation may prevent an organism from performing its normal activities. Or, as is perhaps most common, a mutation may go completely unnoticed.

Let us return to the case of bacterial resistance, a resistance to a substance that was previously lethal. Assume a "normal" situation in which millions of bacterial cells can freely infect man, or any other organism; that is, before the age of antibiotics and sulfa drugs. Assume further that one or two of these millions of bacteria, by chance, are mutated so that they become able to counteract the effect of an antibiotic. Clearly, such a mutation will serve absolutely no purpose, since there is no antibiotic in the vicinity. Thus, the adaptive value, or *survival value,* of this mutation would be *zero.* See Figure 17-B, which shows a family tree through five generations. The method of showing hereditary lines in this way is described in Figure 17-A. Notice, in Figure 17-B, that the mutants may continue surviving in the population just the same.

Now assume a later case, when millions of bacteria are deluged with an antibiotic. If any of these have mutated as described above and resist the drug, then such a change would now have maximum survival value, as shown in Figure 17-C, where all cells that did not mutate in this way could not survive.

In addition, since a bacterial "parent" passes on all of its genetic material, all of the offspring of a mutated bacterial cell will likewise carry the mutated gene, and will, in this example, be resistant to the same antibiotic. This is how a new strain of bacteria is produced. Countless such strains have been described and proved to be produced by mutations. Also proved is that the drugs do not cause the mutations; the mutations occur regardless of the presence or absence of the drugs. Also erroneous, therefore, is the notion that the bacteria "wanted" to change, to mutate in order to protect themselves. A mutation is a random event, occurring solely by chance unless induced purposely by man in his laboratory.

At the other end of the scale, some bacterial mutants have been found which are actually dependent on spe-

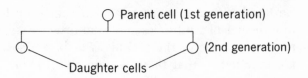

(A) How a bacterial cell divides to form two 'daughter' cells.

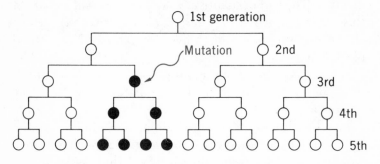

(B) A mutation that renders a bacterial cell resistant to an antibiotic has no advantage in the <u>absence</u> of the antibiotic.

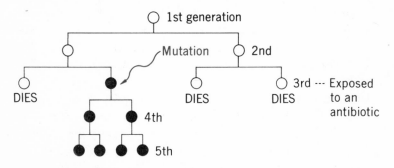

(C) The same mutation has absolute advantage in the <u>presence</u> of the antibiotic.
Only the mutated cells and their offspring can survive, yielding a new strain resistant to the antibiotic.

cific antibiotics. Whereas the previously discussed mutants were merely resistant to the drug, these are
dependent upon it for survival. Obviously, such a mutation is lethal to a bacterial cell that is *not* exposed to the
antibiotic.

Resistance has been observed in higher organisms as
well. In the past twenty years, mutants able to survive
DDT have been found extensively in the house fly and
in body lice. Whereas DDT was very helpful in combat-
ing lice during World War II, it was virtually useless in
the Korean conflict. For another example, there has occurred an increased resistance to DDT sprays by the insects that infest some California citrus orchards.

A final example of the sudden onset of resistance involves the relations of an animal and its parasite; the animal is the European wild rabbit, which became a serious
economic pest in Australia. In 1859, twenty-four wild
rabbits were brought to an estate in the southeast portion
of the isolated continent. By 1928 there were more than
500 million descendants all over the continent. In 1950,
it was decided to spread a virus infection, myxomatosis,
which in three years succeeded in annihilating 80 to 90
percent of the rabbit population. Soon thereafter, however, another increase appeared; a strain of rabbits arose
that was immune to the virus. There is also evidence of
mutation in the virus itself, and strains have formed that
are now less harmful to the rabbits.

Figure 17A. How a bacterial cell divides to form two "daughter"
cells.
Figure 17B. A mutation that renders a bacterial cell resistant to an
antibiotic (black circles) has no advantage in the absence of the
antibiotic.
Figure 17C. The same mutation has absolute advantage in the
presence of the antibiotic. Only the mutated cells and their offspring
can survive, yielding a new strain resistant to the antibiotic.

As Man Learns

With all his directed breeding, man may have "made the scene" in evolution, but he is still an infant in the laboratory of nature. He has learned much about the natural processes of adaptation and evolution. He has even begun, as I have shown, to duplicate some of these processes, and to invent others.

But he has only begun. He has until now applied artificial selection nearly by potluck. Taking the best cattle, the best chickens, the best oranges to become the parents of his hybrids, he has taken advantage of what nature had already produced for him. But the coming explosion of genetic knowledge that is just now beginning to sizzle, as will be shown in Chapter XX, might offer him the opportunities to manufacture his own hybrids of cattle and chickens and oranges, starting from "scratch," from genes which he has produced in a test tube according to his own specifications.

VIII

A Name, a Name.
What's in a Name?

One thing that man does when he arrives on a planet, besides adapting things as he wants to, is to classify what he and nature have caused to adapt.

To see how he does this, kindly close your mind's eye. Imagine you are looking at a hundred different kinds of animals on the street, one animal of each kind. As you scan the organisms before you, your first thought is to compare them. One is the tallest; one the stoutest; one has wings; no, two. Some have legs and some squirm. Some can move, others just sit there. You soon realize that there are traits shared by many of the animals, and there are obvious differences as well.

You are not satisfied with merely calling the animals Number 1, Number 2, Number 100. You want to fit them into categories, subcategories, sub-subcategories, and so on. For example, 34 of them may fit in the category called "legged animals"; of these 34, 20 may have backbones, 14 not. Of the 20 with legs and a backbone, some are meat eaters, others are herbivorous. And so goes the categorization, until each animal becomes the only 1 of the 100 with its own specific list of traits. It may require 10, 20, 50, or even more traits before you can isolate one kind from all the others; but if they are of different kinds, then they are all eventually separable by your classification scheme.

What you have just done is exactly what taxonomists have done in classifying not 100, but about 1,500,000 different animal species and 250,000 plant species. This provides the basis for drawing family trees based on similarities and differences. However, there can arise serious complications. If you discover a new plant, or a new animal, you may not be able to classify it on the spot. You may need to study its entire life cycle and compare many of its traits with those of other plants or animals. Imagine an early taxonomist, centuries ago, trying to classify a tadpole as a member of a frog species; unless he allowed the tadpole to reach adulthood, he would probably have called it a fish.

Now, please close your mind's eye again. This time, imagine that of the 100 different animals you are seeing, each differs from the next by only a single trait. Therefore, if you align some of them as in Figure 18, there will be a difference of one trait between A and B, of two traits between A and C, and so on. A and L would differ from each other by eleven traits. You could hardly tell A and B apart, but you would have no difficulty in differentiating between A and L.

Before we continue, however, realize that such a situation is virtually impossible. Look at yourself and count how many traits you have which your relatives do not have—even within a species, the individual members

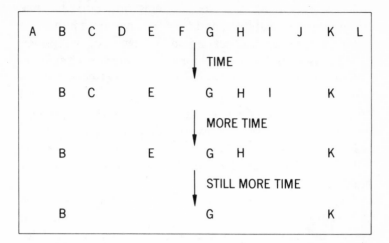

Figure 18. Illustration of how the extinction of some closely related species can simplify the classification of species.

differ by a great deal. But clearly, even if you do not look exactly like your brother, you surely resemble him more than you resemble a frog or a rosebush. This means that you have more genes in common with your brother than you have with a rosebush.

But let us return to our fictitious case of 100 different animal species with a difference of one trait from each animal to the next, as they are lined up there before you. The portion of this parade shown in Figure 18 consists of 12 of the 100 animals. With the situation that is shown on the top row, you would need a good deal of time before you could decide how to categorize your animals. There is so little difference between them that you would probably do one of two things in frustration: you would either fit them all into 1 species, or into 100 different species.

But now, assume further that you are around for a long, long time, and you see all sorts of geologic and climatic

changes occurring; the 100 animals split up, become
adapted to new habitats, and thus become more and more
different from each other. Some species become extinct,
some merge, and some are forced to migrate elsewhere.
You would then see greater differences between the remaining animals. The differences between them would
no longer be in only one trait, but in several, perhaps
very many. This would now permit you to classify more
easily, since the intermediates have become "missing
links," as shown in the second and third rows in the
figure.

Finally, you would have so few animal species before
you, with so sizable the differences between them, that
you would have no problem in telling them apart. This
is the case today, in nature.

Now, to summarize: (1) since organisms mutate; (2)
since natural selection selects some mutated traits and
rejects others; and (3) since organisms therefore tend to
become more and more different from each other as time
goes on; then (4) we can now, today, look at what we
see lined up before us and categorize all living things in
terms of how much they resemble each other—in anatomy, functions, and behaviors.

Therefore, if it were not for evolution, there could be
no classification.

What Names to Use?

Two kinds of biologists concentrate their energies upon
animal and plant differences: systematists and taxonomists. The first group studies the similarities and differences between species, and the second group attempts to
classify species in terms of these similarities and differences.

The taxonomist devises categories. He then assigns living and fossil organisms to these categories according to the traits they possess. Some categories are general rather than specific, and therefore contain very many kinds of organisms. For example, the Kingdom called *Animalia* contains all living and extinct things whose traits permit us to call them "animals," instead of "plants" or anything else. For another example, the Subphylum called *Vertebrata* contains only the animals with backbones.

According to a contemporary view of some systematists, who study not only an organism's form and structure, but its physiology, biochemistry, and behaviors as well, man comes out classified as follows:

Kingdom: *Animal*
  Phylum: *Chordate*
    Subphylum: *Vertebrate*
      Class: *Mammal*
        Order: *Primate*
          Suborder: *Anthropoid*
            Superfamily: *Hominoid*
              Family: *Hominid*
                Genus: *Homo*
                  Species: *Homo sapiens*

The significance of some of these terms will become apparent when we discuss the evolution of man in later chapters.

All organisms are frequently referred to by their species name. The first of the two words is capitalized, and sometimes abbreviated. Thus, *Homo sapiens* is man, *Canis familiaris* is dog, *Rana pipiens* is frog, and *Rana catesbiana* is another kind, or species, of frog.

What Methods to Use?

The methods of the taxonomist have always been rather crude and imperfect and controversial. Even today, if you peruse a dozen different biology textbooks, you may find a dozen different schemes for classifying the animal kingdom.

But taxonomy and systematics are becoming more accurate sciences. There have arisen several techniques that offer exciting promise for the evolutionist. Let us review some of these.

(1) *Antibody analysis.* With the arrival of organ transplantation, the term "rejection" has been popularized. It is now realized that the tissues of one person are slightly different from those of any other person and may reject another's tissues. There are also degrees of difference. Joe's tissue types may resemble Sam's more than they do Harry's. Hence Sam would be a better heart donor for Joe than would Harry.

One reason why animals and plants reject cells foreign to them, obviously, is self-protection. If we could not destroy bacteria easily, for example, we would not live to be born.

Now, if we inject human blood into a rabbit, the rabbit does all it can to get rid of this "foreign" material. To do this, it produces "antibodies" against the foreign blood. These antibodies are specific for human blood; i.e., they will attack only human blood, or blood very closely resembling human blood.

If an animal is closely related to man, its blood will closely resemble man's blood. So if we add the rabbit antibodies against human blood to a chimpanzee's blood in a test tube, we will see a reaction, as we do with human blood. But when we do this with a baboon's blood, the reaction is less severe. And there is no reaction at all with a dog's blood. This indicates that we, or at least our blood, are most closely related to the chimpanzee, next most closely to the baboon, and least related, of these three species, to the dog.

The same technique has been used to determine the taxonomic relationship between goat, beef, dog, and sheep. The goat and sheep appear to be most closely linked; they must then have the most genes in common. Taxonomy has also applied this method in an attempt to classify whales, porcupines, and cattle, as well as plants.

(2) *Protein analysis.* Proteins are perhaps the most important chemical substances in our cells. They are formed according to a *code* stored in our genes. Therefore, protein analysis of different animals should give an indication of how different they are and how different their codes are.

To assist in this task, one systematist has analyzed the egg-white proteins of over 2,000 species of birds. Using refined techniques, the systematist could quite easily spot very slight differences between any two proteins. Very slight differences in protein makeups could indicate corresponding gene differences. These differences could then be used to build a family tree of the organisms investigated. The method has also been used to show that the pig is much closer to the whale than to the cow, horse, or sheep, contrary to what one might expect.

(3) *Behavioral analysis.* What we do, and what all animals do, is called "behavior." Much of it can be measured. Taxonomists are just now beginning to look to behavior analysis in order to classify animals. For example, slight differences in courtship songs in frogs, as well as in birds, could indicate slight gene differences. The latter could indicate the evolutionary relationships of the animals studied.

(4) *Genetic analysis.* With the rapid advance in technology, scientists are proposing that we learn to go directly to the genes, thereby bypassing the antibodies, the proteins, and behaviors, to study differences between species. This could clarify immediately many questions not now answerable.

We have seen that organisms can be classified because they have evolved to become more and more different from each other; a polarization occurs whereby in-between stages either differentiate or become extinct. We now need to survey the processes by which organisms do become different, do adapt at times, and do evolve.

IX

But You Still Haven't Told Me How Things Begin.

We have seen that biological evolution is, in part, the adaptation of organisms to their environment. But what does this really mean? How is adaptation achieved? We can say that a monkey adapts, but what is it that adapts? Its brain? Its toenails? Its genes?

Further, it is one thing to say that a frog has adapted to its environment; but it is quite another thing to say that its ancestors evolved into turtles.

How can the members of a species achieve a gradual change in color, size, mating behavior, speed, or internal functions? And incidentally, is it the *members* of a species that undergo gradual change, or is it the *species* to which they belong? And what is the difference between these alternatives?

These questions are difficult to answer, but are now generally answerable. To explain the process of evolutionary change, it is necessary first to describe some of the properties of a population of plants or animals. A *population* is a local group of animals, or of plants, of the same species. For example, if you drive from Maine to Oregon, you can see a series of forests, with pine trees in many of them. Although the pine trees may belong to the same species, they are separated into many local populations.

When populations living in different areas are exposed to differing environments, different adaptations can result. Such slight differences, when they continue to accumulate, can eventually produce groups so different from each other that they belong not only to different populations, but to different species.

The Population Gene Pool

Now, imagine that you are observing a population of apple trees in an orchard, or a population of earthworms in the soil of your backyard, or of mosquitoes around a swamp, or of people in a town. And imagine that you cannot see trees or worms or mosquitoes or people. Instead, all you can see are their genes, the many genes within their many cells.

Since one person may have 100,000 genes in each of his cells, and since he may have 10 trillion cells in his body, you may be seeing 1 quintillion genes for each person. If there are 100 people in the town, you do not see 100 people, but 100 quintillion genes.

All of the "human" genes in that town collectively constitute a *gene pool*. Other gene pools are those of the earthworms, of the apple trees, and of the mosquitoes. Some of these pools may be slowly changing in makeup, since all genes are subject to change. As mentioned earlier, changes in genes are called *mutations.*

To understand the effect of a gene mutation on a gene pool, we must first know what is a gene. In most of our body's cells there is a *nucleus;* it contains rod-shaped structures called *chromosomes.* Our somatic cells have forty-six such chromosomes, arranged in twenty-three pairs. Within the chromosomes are found the genes, linked together in a "chain." Most genes contain a code which carries a "message."

What does the cell do with its many codes? As stated earlier, any one cell uses very few of its genes; most are turned off. A liver cell has no need to use the genes responsible for eye color, for example. But the genes that are used permit the manufacture of proteins.

Proteins are of many types; most are enzymes that regulate the chemistry of the cell. But others assist in other functions, such as oxygen-carrying by the blood, stretching of muscles, seeing, digesting foods, and so on. Indeed, much of what animals and plants do, much of what they are, depends on what proteins their cells can produce.

And what kinds of proteins their cells can produce depend on the kinds of genes they have.

Therefore, the genes in its chromosomes make a cow a cow, instead of a dog or a tree; genes make a frog different from a worm, or a person, or a begonia. A hen and a rooster produce a baby of that same species because they pass the correct genes to their baby. So does man and every other living species.

In species that reproduce by the mating of two partners—sexual reproduction—as in man and most plants and animals, the "baby" receives a mixture of two codes, one from Mom and one from Dad. Because it *is* a mixture, the baby becomes slightly different from its parents;

but not different enough to become part of a different species. You may be two inches taller than your parents, or your eyes may be blue and theirs brown, or your front teeth may be slightly shorter than theirs, or your blood may require a few seconds more to clot than theirs does, but you are still very human.

In species that do not reproduce by the mating of partners, but simply by the splitting of one cell into two "daughter cells"—asexual reproduction—the babies usually acquire the very same code as "Mom" had, and therefore look exactly like her, barring any mutation. In fact, they *are* "Mom," now split into two "twins." This is the case in the ameba, in bacteria, and in many other lower forms of life.*

Now here is the important point: sexually reproducing species produce *differences* each time they produce a new generation. The offspring are slightly different from the parents. Therefore, these species can evolve faster for reasons that will soon become obvious to the reader.

The discovery of gene action, of how a gene transfers its code to the protein-building factories outside the nucleus, has been the bulwark of the evolution theory. To say that some species can progressively adapt to an environment was rather conjectural until the chemistry of gene action was determined.

In summary then, the structures, functions, and behaviors of organisms are largely due to the kinds of genes inherited by them. The environment can also affect structures, functions, and behaviors; but we are here surveying the evolution of *species*, of gene pools as they are passed on from generation to generation. Any change that a population undergoes, if it can be passed on, is a change undergone by its genes; any change induced by the en-

* See *Sex and the Single Cell* by Dolores Elaine Keller in this BSCS series.

vironment on one member or more remains with that member. If I have my appendix removed, my offspring will still be born with an appendix. But if a sex cell mutates in such a way as to prevent the "appendix" genes from expressing themselves, then my offspring could conceivably be born without an appendix.

If an insect species came to resemble a thorn, or if a flower came to resemble a female bee, it is because each generation produced offspring slightly different from the parents. The long-term "choice" of nature was in favor of changes that progressively made the insect more able to "hide," or the flower more able to "fake."

Changes in the Gene Pool

Let us now reduce the number of genes we are observing in our town of 100 people. Instead of looking at 100 quintillion genes, all the genes in this local human gene pool, let us imagine that we see only those genes responsible for one trait; say, one kind of protein in a cell.

For example, if we look at one liver cell per person, and look at the 2 genes in that cell that are responsible for the production of an enzyme needed for sugar storage, we then see only 200 genes in the town. We disregard all the others.

Some of these 200 genes will be dominant, and some will be recessive. However, it is important to understand that when this species originated, all of the genes for this one trait were identical; there was no question of dominance or of recessiveness. Sometime after its origin, however, a mutation occurred that altered a gene slightly. But this slight change was sufficient to render it different from the others, making this gene either dominant or recessive in relation to the others.

So by the time of our story, the 200 genes are of two kinds, either dominant or recessive. It would be said, therefore, that there are two forms of this gene.

Now let us say that 150 of the 200 genes are of the dominant form, and 50 are of the recessive. If this ratio remains constant for a long time, the population is said to be in *genetic equilibrium* as far as this one kind of gene is concerned. This means that as long as no other mutations occur, and as long as the town's people mate at random (perhaps a moral breakdown to our analogy), the numbers, or *frequencies,* of the two forms will probably remain constant, generation after generation after generation.

In this case, the frequency of the dominant gene is 75 percent (150 out of 200), and that of the recessive is 25 percent (50 out of 200).

If the population is evolving, or changing in any way, such as by the migration of its members to other towns, then the frequencies of some gene forms will change.

Mutation: Change in Gene Chemistry

The sampling of populations over a series of generations usually shows that gene pools do not remain in equilibrium. One of the factors that upsets the equilibrium is gene mutation.

Mutations occur at random and are, very simply, changes in the chemistry of the hereditary material. If they occur in somatic cells, they affect only the individual involved, and not future gene pools. However, if they occur in sex cells, such as sperm, egg, or pollen, they can be transmitted to later generations.

Mutation is the chief agent that introduces *variation* into a gene pool. AND VARIATION IS ABSOLUTELY

NECESSARY for the normal operation of natural selection. Please reread the last sentence; it is very important.

If all members of a population had the same forms of a gene—for example, if all human beings had type O blood—then nature could not "select" and no evolution could occur, under normal circumstances. To exemplify this point more carefully: if all foxes were exactly identical, then none would have an advantage over the others. Instead of evolving, the population would be static and unchanging. This would be fine if the individual foxes were each able to catch a rabbit for dinner. But if none of the foxes could run fast enough, then they would all starve to death.

What happens, at least in our story, is that some foxes are just slightly faster than others, hence they win the race and get the food. They are obviously more likely to survive long enough to produce offspring, thus passing their "speed" genes to the next generation. Therefore, the next generation comes out to be slightly faster than the previous one, on the average. And on goes the process of adaptation. But it is an adaptation of a gene pool, and not of its individual members. A particular fox is either "fast" or "slow," and probably cannot change. But one generation, one gene pool, can be faster than the previous one; just as one generation of human teenagers can be taller than the previous one.

Mutation, then, creates variation, and variation permits adaptation. And, as we shall see, adaptation permits evolution.

When a mutation first appears in a gene pool, a heterozygous condition of the affected genes results: dominant and recessive genes. If an organism has the genes *AA* for a trait and one of the genes mutates to become recessive to the other, the organism will then have the genes *Aa* in the cell where the mutation occurred. Only if the gene

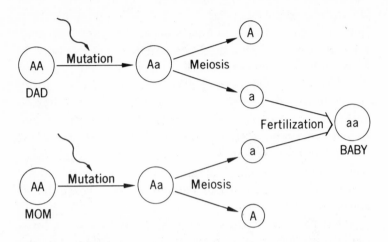

Figure 19. Process by which a recessive gene produced by mutation can become homozygous and expressive.

a becomes more frequent in the gene pool, by other mutations in other individuals, can an offspring become homozygous *aa*. This can occur, as shown in Figure 19, for example, in the mating of two heterozygous parents, *Aa*, who each produce two kinds of sex cells. Some of the sex cells have the *A* gene, some the *a* gene. If the two sex cells with *a* fertilize, the resulting offspring will be *aa*.

The results of a mutation can sometimes be tragic. In the human species, for example, there are at least thirty-three known hereditary disorders in which the protein responsible for the error has been identified, including PKU, albinism, and gout. There are in all more than a thousand other hereditary disorders not yet fully understood. Indeed, the gene mutations that cause the production of abnormal proteins are very real, and sometimes experienced very painfully.*

* See *Human Heredity and Birth Defects* by E. Peter Volpe in this BSCS series.

If we wish ever to eliminate hereditary disorders altogether, we will probably have to strike at their source, the gene. What then is a gene, exactly, and what happens when it mutates? To explain, I will first describe the gene in more detail than before. As I do so, the reader might profit from an occasional glance at Figure 20-A.

A gene is a small segment of a long chemical molecule called DNA. A truly amazing fact is that most of the genes in the biosphere, in plants, and in animals, are built partly of the same four kinds of basic blocks, called *nitrogen bases*. We may label the four by the letters *A, T, C,* and *G,* the initial letters of the bases (adenine, thymine, cytosine, and guanine).

In most organisms, each chromosome consists of *two* intertwining DNA chains; the two strands are tied together by their nitrogen bases. But the bases can join only in specific ways: *A* can join only with *T,* and *C* with *G.* As we shall see, this specific union is what constitutes the "code" so often referred to in this chapter.

The code operates as shown in Figure 20-A. When a gene is "turned on," that area of the twisted DNA chain untwists, and the bases on one strand attract matching bases, which are flowing alone nearby. Wherever there is a *C* base in the DNA strand, a *G* matches with it; and all *As* attract *U* bases. (In the "messenger" which forms, *T* is replaced by *U,* uracil.)

Thus, a copy of the gene is made, but not an exact copy; it is more analogous to a photographic "negative." The copy, the "messenger," leaves the chromosome and migrates to another region of the cell to direct the formation of protein segments.

What this means is that the messenger directs the *order* in which amino acids will be linked together. Therefore, the order of bases in DNA regulates the order of amino acids in proteins.

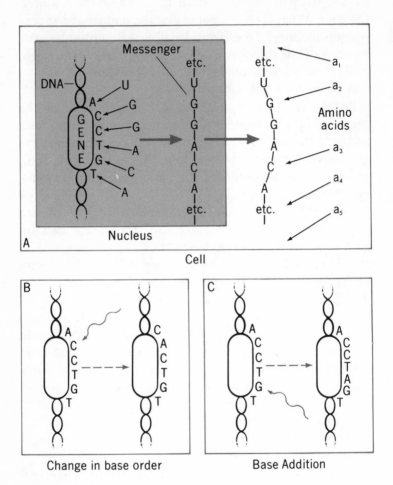

Figure 20A. Relationship of cell code to protein buildup.
Figure 20B. Example of gene mutation: Change in base order.
Figure 20C. Example of gene mutation: Addition of an extra base.

A gene mutation, then, could consist of a change in the order of bases in a gene; this could lead to minor, or to very drastic, changes in the resulting messenger and the resulting protein (Figure 20-B). A mutation could also be the result of an addition of a base into the DNA chain, the replacement of one base by another, or the removal of a base (Figure 20-C).

One example that illustrates how serious can be even a minor change in the code, or in a protein, is that of sickle-cell anemia discussed earlier. The condition is characterized by a substitution of only 1 out of 300 amino acids in one small part of the affected protein. A change of 1 amino acid out of 300 can cause people to die!

However, some mutations produce changes which increase the chances of survival of their owners. And it is these that provide the major impetus to the evolutionary

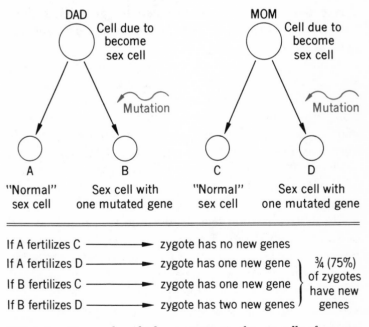

Figure 21. Manner by which a mutation in the sex cells of parents can become incorporated into the offspring.

process. Such owners, being slightly more able to survive than their non-mutated brothers, may then pass the new traits to their offspring.

But it is important to remember that in a sexually reproducing organism, the product of a mutation cannot be passed on to another generation *unless* the mutation occurred in a sex cell, and unless it is that sex cell that is fertilized. Therefore, the chance that a mutation product, namely a modified protein, be "seized" by nature is slight indeed. Most mutations occur in somatic cells, as would be expected since there are so many more of them.

How Often Do Gene Mutations Occur?

The genes that have been studied by geneticists show more or less constant *mutation rates,* whether in somatic cells or in sex cells.

A mutation rate can be defined in one of two ways. First, if we wish to stress only one set of genes, that set responsible for only one trait, the mutation rate is "the number of such genes that will mutate in a total of 100,000 sex cells" in the gene pool. The number is usually very low. For example, the genes that determine if corn seeds are colored or not have an average mutation rate of about 49 mutations per 100,000 sex cells. In man, the condition known as "fetal rickets," which produces abnormally short arms and legs, is also due to a mutation and occurs in 1 child out of every 12,000; since it takes two parents to produce a child, this means that the mutation rate for this condition is 1 per 24,000 sex cells; or about 4 per 100,000 sex cells. Hemophilia has a rate of 3 per 100,000, and sickle-cell anemia of 1,000 per 100,000 in the American Negro population.

A second method of expressing mutation rates is to disregard specific genes, but to look instead at all genes, for all traits combined. For example, in some fruit flies there is a mutation rate of one gene mutation per every twenty sex cells. This means that if we look at *all* the genes in all the sex cells in a fruit fly's gene pool, one of the genes, any one, will mutate in every group of twenty sex cells.

Each of us has two to four mutant genes which arose during sex cell formation in our parents. To these we add our own, plus the ones that our parents inherited. In fact, 50 percent of all sex cells produced by a person bear at least one new mutated gene. That means, as shown in Figure 21, that 75 percent of all pregnancies yield a child bearing at least one mutated gene. The gene could be useful, detrimental, or unnoticed.

You might ask, however, how long it takes for mutations really to change things, if they occur so rarely, and if the changes they cause are usually so slight.

One investigator, George Gaylord Simpson, arbitrarily selecting one trait, has devised a simple mathematical model to show how very small, rare, seemingly insignificant changes in a trait can result in large-scale evolution over a long period of time. Let us outline his approach.

(1) Perhaps the best-known evolutionary phenomenon is that of the horse, which originated 60 million years ago, at which time it was only ten inches high.

(2) Assuming that 15 million generations of horse ancestors have elapsed since that time, Simpson estimates that there have been 1,500 billion individual horses in this long ancestry.

(3) He assumes that in all that time, 300,000 favorable mutations have occurred in the size of a ridge on the upper molar tooth. By "favorable" we mean that the

mutation was apt to increase the survival ability of horses; as far as this one trait is concerned, fossil evidence shows that the ridge increased in size to suit a changing diet.

(4) Not all of the 300,000 favorable mutations produced "new" genes. They may have produced a trait "new" to one horse, but already "seen" in the gene pool, by other horses. Assuming that I become subject to a favorable mutation, the result is "new" to me, but I may not be the first person in town to experience this change. Therefore, the investigator assumes that only 300 of the 300,000 favorable mutations were genuine "firsts"; that is only 0.1 percent.

(5) If we divide the 60 million years of horse evolution into these 300 "new" steps, that means that on the average one "step" occurred every 200,000 years.

(6) The next question is: How much of an increase in ridge height occurred at each step? Based on the known height of the ridge 60 million years ago and the height of the same ridge in the modern horse, we know that it lengthened by about an inch. An increase of one inch in 60 million years! Therefore, each "step" increased the ridge height by 1/300 of an inch.

Now then, if horses were evolutionists, no horse could have perceived such a small change in its own generation, for an obvious reason: in its own lifetime, if the horse had sampled the ridge heights of all other living horses of its generation, it would have found a range of about an eighth of an inch. The *range* in heights was then far greater, at any one time, than the overall change in the *average* height from one generation to the next.

To conclude this section, it must be noted that in addition to gene mutations, whole chromosome mutations can occur whereby a chromosome may be separated into pieces, the pieces rejoining abnormally, or remaining separated. Also, when sex cells are formed, some chromo-

number in a cell. This can have severe repercussions. For
example, one form of human mongolism is characterized
by the presence of forty-seven, not the usual forty-six,
chromosomes in all of the individual's somatic cells.

Perhaps many evolutionary events have been caused by
chromosome mutations. But it is generally believed that
most adaptations occur rather by the slower, often less
obvious, gene mutations.

Drift and Flow: Change in Gene Frequencies

It is obvious by now that gene pools are constantly subject to change. Most changes are probably "lost in the
crowd," especially if the population is in genetic equilibrium, or is not facing strong pressures to change.

The more or less regular appearance of new genes produces differences upon which the population can capital-
ize. But besides mutating, and being subjected to natural
selection, a gene pool may change in other ways.

In a town of 100 people, assume that a few new residents arrive from the next town. Such a migration of
genes into the already established pool can alter the "balance of power" significantly, as when a motorcycle gang
hits town. Known as *gene flow,* migration into or away
from a gene pool can subject the remaining genes to selection pressures that are different from those already
established by centuries of adaptation. Therefore, a significant evolutionary factor is the amount of migration
to which a gene pool is subjected.

Another, and probably even more significant, factor is
genetic drift. This is defined as the random isolation of
"neighborhoods," or portions, of the population. Usually,

if a flood or avalanche isolates some organisms, you would
expect the isolated group to possess gene frequencies that
are different from the frequencies in the larger parent
population.

Look at it this way: If you toss 100 pennies onto a
table, you may get 60 heads and 40 tails—a 6 to 4 ratio.
Then close your eyes and select 10 of the pennies on the
table; if you should get 6 heads and 4 tails—the same ratio—you would "flip." The chance that you would select
a ratio *other* than 6 to 4 is much greater.

Similarly, if some organisms become separated from the
rest, the chances are slim indeed that the frequencies of
genes in the isolated group are identical to those of the
parent group.

For another example, assume that some Europeans wish
to migrate to America and that they are the first to come
to this continent. This is an example of a *gene flow*. But
assume that the blood types of all people living in Europe are distributed this way: 40 percent of them have
type O blood, 40 percent type A, and the rest have types
B and AB; but in the emigrant group, to assume an extreme, everyone has type O blood. The frequency of O
blood in America would then be 100 percent, and not 40
percent. And this drastic change was achieved by one
simple act—the boarding of a ship.

Such a gene flow in which the frequencies of gene
forms are changed is what we call *genetic drift*. It can
have a sizable evolutionary effect. But since drift is random, and not influenced by natural selection, the results
are not always beneficial.

For example, assume that a trait is represented by not
two, but four forms of a gene in a gene pool. The gene
forms in our story will be A_1, A_2, A_3, and A_4. If the population is large, and if there are equal numbers of all possible combinations of these four forms, then there would

result *ten* possible kinds of combinations, as shown aligned in the top row in Figure 22. Each of the four genes has a frequency of 25 percent, since each occurs five times in the gene pool of twenty genes.

Now, assume that seven of the ten animals are killed by a flash flood, and that the three remaining animals have these genes: A_1A_1, A_1A_4, and A_3A_4. Then, the frequencies resulting from this genetic drift would be as shown in the figure. (It must be emphasized that most cases of genetic drift are much slower than the cata-

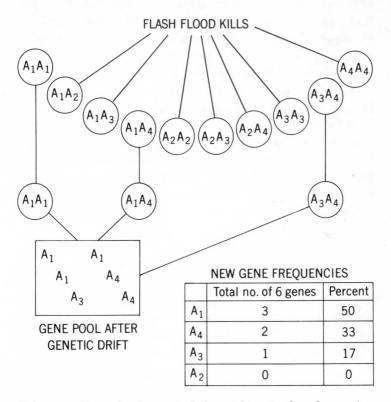

Figure 22. Example of genetic drift, resulting in altered gene frequencies.

strophic isolation caused by our flash flood, but the results can be the same.)

If genes A_2 and A_3 were not too helpful to the species, then nature would now have taken a rapid step forward; it is simpler to remove A_3 at 17 percent frequency than at 25 percent frequency.

Also, natural selection did not have to work for years to remove A_2. Genetic drift removed the gene in one clean sweep.

In a reverse situation, assume that gene A_1 is very detrimental and had already begun to take its toll, to eat away at the population, by the time of the sampling in the figure. If A_1 had such an adverse influence at 25 percent frequency, imagine how great an impact it could have when suddenly jumping to a 50 percent frequency.

It is important to remember that the effect of a gene on the organisms in a gene pool can be modified drastically if its frequency, or that of other genes, changes. This is because a gene does not work independently of other genes, but in relation to them, as will be explained later. Therefore, gene flow and genetic drift can have sizable effects on what is left behind, as well as on what is flowing or drifting.

The Maintenance Crew: Recombination

Thus far we have seen that mutations are the original source of variation, and that the frequencies of different genes can be altered by gene flow and genetic drift.

But there is another factor that plays a far-ranging role in the maintenance of variation in a population. This is *genetic recombination*.

Everytime a sex cell is produced, it undergoes a very

complicated process of cell division. During this process, the individual chromosomes join, each with its partner. While the two are paired, they do an odd but evolutionarily important thing. They trade some genes. The resulting exchange produces two "new" chromosomes, each with a combination of its own genes and genes from its partner. This is what is called *genetic recombination.* The process that makes it possible is called *crossing over,* and is shown occurring at two points between segments of paired chromosomes in Figure 23-B; a comparison of Figures 23-A and 23-C shows how crossing over yields chromosomes with modified gene sequences.

Much as people are affected by their social entourage, so is a gene affected by its neighboring genes on the same chromosomes in the production of protein.

As an illustration of this, picture a gene called B_1 on a chromosome, with gene A_1 on one side of it and gene C_1

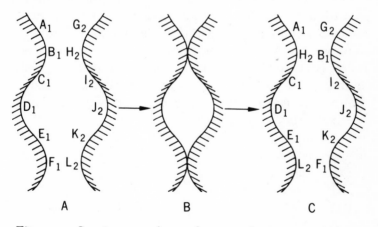

Figure 23. Crossing-over of genes between chromosomes. (A) Segments of two chromosomes, with each letter representing a gene. (B) Contacts are made. (C) Same segments, showing modified gene sequences.

on the other side. If this $A_1B_1C_1$ combination has survived the sieve of natural selection, then it is probably quite satisfactory, perhaps even crucial, for survival.

Assume, however, that genetic recombination between this chromosome and its partner, which has genes A_2, B_2, and C_2, yields a new combination that reads $A_1B_2C_1$. If it turns out that this combination is very slightly more beneficial than the previous $A_1B_1C_1$ combination, then nature may select for it. After several generations this may become an established combination in the gene pool.

Therefore, in our story, a past mutation had changed gene B_1 into B_2. The latter gene was then available, so to speak. If its best partners are A_1 and C_1, and if recombination ever matches it with these, then natural selection has a new combination to experiment with, and perhaps to maintain for posterity.

We could call $A_1B_2C_1$ a new evolutionary step.

To summarize, although mutation is the primary source of variation, genetic recombination is by far the most influential source of persisting variation. Recombination must work with whatever genes the mutation provides, but it is recombination that keeps shuffling these genes around. Since the shuffling of genes affects their activity, then nature is constantly being provided with new combinations from which to select.

We now have the following list of agents influential in gene pool changes, that is, in evolution:

(1)   gene and chromosome mutations,
(2)   gene flow and genetic drift,
(3)   genetic recombination.

X

Can a Cat Become a Dog?

Gene pool variation permits the slow adaptation of local populations to their environments. But that is a far cry from stating that one species of animal or plant can become a different species, unable to breed with the former species. Can a dog become a cat? Can a fish change into a frog? Can an ape become a man? We are now in a different ball park. In fact, we are playing a different game.

Or are we?

Could the process of *speciation* not be different from adaptation, but just another kind of adaptation? Could a new species arise when a local population has remained isolated from nearby populations so long that it has become more and more different from these, one difference being in its reproductive organs?

Differences can arise, through the process of adaptation, not only in behavior, liver functions, tooth size, and so on, but in reproductive organs as well. If two populations of the same species have been separated long enough and cannot interbreed when and if they meet again, will they then be of two different species?

To answer these questions, we must of course define the term species. Two methods exist. Some define the members of a species by their appearance: The members of one species are all recognizably similar in outward appearance. This could be called the "museum" definition of species. Others, namely geneticists and evolutionists, define a species as a group of organisms able to breed together and to produce similar offspring who are also able to interbreed. This definition stresses the ability to reproduce as the main criterion. For present purposes, let us accept the second definition.

What then could constitute speciation, the formation of a species? We could define this process as the gradual transformation of some members of a species so that they can no longer breed with other members not transformed.

The key factor would be the inability of separated groups of a species to interbreed. Whatever differences accumulate in separated groups during the period of separation would be dissolved, mixed, if the group should rejoin and be able to interbreed.

Therefore:

Adaptation results mainly from
    (1)   mutation,
    (2)   flow and drift,
    (3)   recombination.
But the adaptation called "speciation" results mainly from
    (1)   mutation,
    (2)   flow and drift,
    (3)   recombination,
    (4)   reproductive isolation.

Isolation: How to Form a Species

It may take around 50,000 years for two isolated populations of a species to become new and distinct species. This is a rough estimate, and is quite variable and difficult to ascertain. But it offers a guideline.

Among the major mechanisms by which reproductive isolation may lead to species formation are the following:

(1) *Space barriers.* Geographical isolation of the fragments of a population is the most common cause of speciation. The best site for such a study is an island; and the Hawaiian Islands, because of their age, offer an ideal site. The oldest of these are 5.6 million years old; the youngest, the island of Hawaii itself, is 700,000 years old. Studies in fruit fly speciation have enabled evolutionists to trace the precise ancestries of a number of species. It was discovered that some species could have arisen from *one* pregnant female fruit fly that migrated to an island. This is the extreme in genetic drift, where the genetic makeups of only two individuals determine the future of an entire area's gene pool. The female's eggs and her mate's sperm create, in effect, a new population. This is not the normal course of events, however.

(2) *Temporal barriers.* Occasionally, different populations of a species adopt different seasons or times of day for breeding. If two isolated populations of one flower species adapt to their slightly different environments by changing their flowering times, even by a few spring days, they cannot produce offspring, even if the winds transfer pollen from one population to the other.

(3) *Behavioral barriers.* In many species of animals, perhaps in most, specific mating rituals have evolved; without these, reproduction might not occur. Any deviation from them may result in the failure to copulate. The

rituals include specific motions, mating calls, discharges from scent glands, and temporary coloration. If two adjacent, but partially isolated populations come to modify their mating behavior even slightly, intersterility can result. One sex fails to recognize the other. This has been shown, for example, in frogs. Although nearly identical, the mating calls of male frogs of various kinds living in the same pond have been analyzed carefully and found to be slightly different in pitch and frequency. These differences often are enough to maintain and to increase the reproductive isolation between populations.

(4) *Mechanical barriers.* Just as bones, teeth, blood, skin, wings, and noses can become progressively different in evolutionary time, so can the sex cells or sex organs involved in reproduction. Such changes are the most obvious and most direct causes of reproductive isolation.

For example, if copulating organs become slightly different, as has been found in adjacent populations of fruit flies, mosquitoes, and salamanders, mating might be impossible. Or mating might occur, but the male sperm may not be tolerated by the female reproductive tract. Also, even if sperm and egg do fertilize, the resulting zygote may die sooner or later. Finally, even if born, the offspring may be sterile, thereby unable to pass on its hybrid mixture of traits. There are *degrees* of sterility between different populations of animals; it is not an all-or-none phenomenon.

Perhaps the most studied case of reproductive interfertility has been that of the common leopard frog, found all the way from Vermont to Mexico. Many of the studies have shown that adjacent populations, not separated for as long as some distant populations, can produce normal offspring. But the more remote the populations in nature, the higher the degree of sterility. It is not inconceivable, a few hundred years from now, that biologists will refer to the different populations as different species if they become completely intersterile.

Figure 24 depicts a possible scheme by which speciation may occur. As the reader proceeds through the stages, he should notice the frequencies of the different shapes shown, and how these frequencies change from stage to

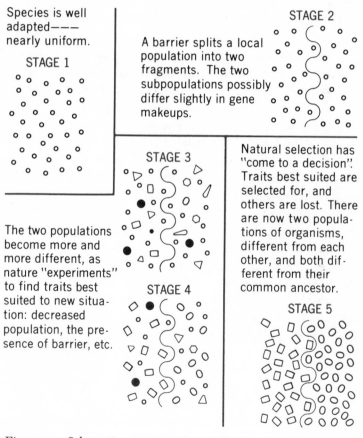

Species is well adapted——— nearly uniform.

STAGE 1

STAGE 2

A barrier splits a local population into two fragments. The two subpopulations possibly differ slightly in gene makeups.

STAGE 3

The two populations become more and more different, as nature "experiments" to find traits best suited to new situation: decreased population, the presence of barrier, etc.

STAGE 4

Natural selection has "come to a decision". Traits best suited are selected for, and others are lost. There are now two populations of organisms, different from each other, and both different from their common ancestor.

STAGE 5

Figure 24. Schematic representation of the process of speciation.

stage. The numbering of stages and the scheme described is purely arbitrary; it is one example of how speciation *could* occur.

Biologists have a name for instances where a certain trait, reproductive or otherwise, is seen to change very slightly, but very definitely, in different populations of the same, or related, plant or animal species. The gradual change in one trait—for example, from north to south along the globe—is called a *cline*.

As an illustration, look at "stage 5" in Figure 24. Assume that the two isolated groups are entirely alike in every respect except that one group consists of square individuals and the other of oval individuals. The manner in which they came to be different in this one trait involves the processes illustrated in stages 1 through 5. But forget stages 1 to 4 for now. You happen upon a field and find, on either side of a barrier, the two populations seen in stage 5. You would then turn to your partner and say: "See the cline?" One difference, due to adaptation to different environments.

For specific examples, let us look at fox ears as shown in Figure 25-A. Fox ears are smaller in warmer, southern climates than in northern areas; the cline is depicted in the figure for three foxes from three areas. For another example, the leg stripes on zebras become denser along a path shown in Figure 25-B. Also, the human body is, on the average, larger and stouter in northern areas (the Eskimo) than in the south, where it is tall and lean (the African Negro): adaptations to local environments. Eskimos and African Negroes can still mate (but geographic

Figure 25A. Heads of arctic fox, red fox, and desert fox, showing cline in ear size.
Figure 25B. Cline in the striping of zebra legs, from different regions of South Africa.

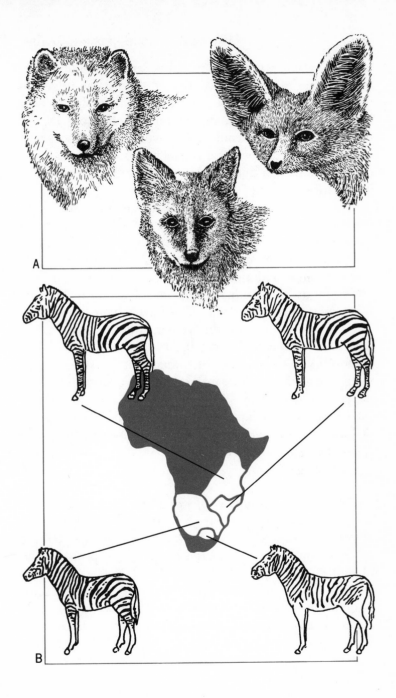

A

B

isolation usually prevents it), they are still interfertile, because the cline in which they differ is not in reproductive organs, but in body stature. If they should ever become adaptively different in reproductive organs, for example, then there could arise two different species of men. But that has become a virtual impossibility in our age of communication and transportation and lowered racial boundaries.

Clines undoubtedly exist for many, many traits, since a species that migrates from a central point becomes more and more isolated from that point and is subjected to more and more different environments. But the differences are often gradual and not abrupt. The process is perhaps analogous to the gradual distortion of a tale making its way across a neighborhood. The farther you travel from the original source of the rumor, the more different, spicy, and detrimental it may become.

Obviously, the degrees of intersterility described previously constitute clines of reproductive organs, or behaviors, or functions. We may be accurate in stating, then, that when adaptations are in reproductive organs, or functions, or behaviors, they may cause the process of speciation to occur.

Another Maintainer of Variation: Polyploidy

We must mention another factor evident in maintaining the variation necessary to the evolutionary process—the phenomenon of *polyploidy*. As stated earlier, most organisms have two sets of chromosomes in all somatic cells, a condition called *diploidy*. The organisms of some species, however, have more than two sets; they may have three complete sets, or more. In fact, the species of Spring Beauty plants has fifty different kinds of plants, with 50 known chromosome numbers ranging from 12 per cell to 191 per cell. Polyploidy is the only known process by which a new species can arise in one or two generations, suddenly and without reproductive isolation. It is much more common in plants than in animals; one estimate is that nearly half of all flowering plants are polyploids. Among animals, certain salamanders and fruit flies are polyploids.

Polyploidy has produced many of our valuable crop plants: wheat, oats, potatoes, corn, bananas, coffee, tobacco, sugar cane—all these and more owe their origins to this explosive evolutionary event.

The event occurs during a faulty cell division process whereby the chromosomes are not divided evenly between two sex cells. If chromosomes divide over and over again, but the cell itself does not, one sex cell can have more than its normal number of chromosomes. The resulting increase in the number of genes can have sizable effects on the offspring. Polyploids that do produce offspring produce some that are sterile, or some that are fertile, depending on the species.

The condition has been produced artificially with corn, tomato, and onion plants. One experimenter soaked onion roots in colchicine for four days. The result: more than 1,000 chromosomes per cell!

Polyploidy must therefore be added to the list as a significant cause of variation in plants. It is not classified as a chromosome mutation because the chromosomes themselves generally do not change. But it does add to variation, as does sexual recombination. Because it is relatively uncommon in aminal, it is probably not a factor of great importance.

And Another Maintainer of Variation: Hybridization

A factor already mentioned, and one that is important to some extent in the evolutionary process, is hybridization between two different species.

If two species can be crossed, and if the offspring are able to reproduce, then new kinds of plants or animals can result. This is, as is polyploidy, another rapid method of evolutionary change.

If you cross a radish with a cabbage, you can obtain a hybrid called a "radocabbage"; it is fertile and produces similar baby radocabbages.

If you cross a male donkey with a female horse, you get a mule. A cross between a female donkey and a male horse yields a hinny. Male mules and male hinnies are sterile; but the females of either hybrid are fertile. Female mule × male donkey = mule; female mule × male horse = horse.

If you cross . . . and the list goes on.

A Poem of Nature: Summing It All Up

Nature has evolved its own system of checks and balances for selecting and maintaining the gene combinations best suited to their environments.

Because there are: mutation, recombination, polyploidy, and fertile hybridization,
       then there is: variation.
Because there is: variation,
       then there can be: natural selection.
Because there is: selection,
      then there is; adaptation.
And because there is adaptation, there can be speciation.

This scheme is oversimplified; but it is generally true. A brief scientific poem may clarify the picture.

> What Mutation instigates
> Recombination escalates.
> What Selection confiscates
> Isolation speciates.

Now Then: What IS Evolution?

We still have not defined evolution.

Clearly, evolution is that process by which some properties of a group render it more adaptable to its environment. This applies to galaxies, stars, planets, atmospheres, continents, and all living things.

But this chapter was restricted to one kind of evolution: the evolution of living things, that is, biological evolution.

We may define biological evolution as: changes in the gene frequencies of a gene pool whereby (1) the species becomes better adapted to its environment, and (2) said changes are transmitted to subsequent generations.

Biological evolution is an evolution of gene pools, of populations, and not of organisms, although the latter may benefit from the evolutionary process. I was born with my share of genes, given me by millions of years of evolution and adapted by my environment; and at the moment, there is nothing I can do to change these genes. I cannot evolve. But the gene pool of which I am a part can evolve, and is apparently doing so.

Biological evolution is not only the maintenance and propagation of beneficial gene combinations, but it is also the removal of harmful gene combinations. Therefore, the topic of this book is not solely one of progress, but of a combination of progression and regression; of building, breaking down, and reconstructing.

It is as if we saw a train riding by. Its shape, its parts, its velocity are all there for us to see or determine. We may hop on for the ride and enjoy the luxury of being alive, but without the proper tools we cannot change that upon which we ride. The train is the gene pool, primarily that gene pool portion consisting of sex cells. The tools will be developed in the future by the genetic engineer.

It is easy to see why the concept of evolution was initially the sole property of the philosopher. But it later became part and parcel of biology. It is now shared with the chemist and the mathematician as well. Since gene changes are chemical changes, the biologist must depend on the chemist for many answers. And since population dynamics such as genetic drift and gene flow are largely statistical, the mathematician has become incorporated into the research team as well.

XI

And Incidentally, How DID Life Begin?

You don your breathing mask quickly. But you are so intrigued by what is happening before you that you forget to jot down some notes for posterity.

You are witnessing the origin of life!

As you stand on the cliff's edge, looking down upon the crevices below, you begin to feel the tingle of perspiration along your back. The atmosphere above you consists mainly of superheated water vapor, and it has no free oxygen for you to breathe. This hot environment is causing some simple chemicals to become elaborated into methane gas, another gas called hydrogen cyanide, and another called ammonia.

After a while, the combination of some of the water vapor, ammonia, and methane produces other chemicals still more complicated. All this is occurring in the atmosphere above you. But as the Earth and its atmosphere begin to cool, you can witness in the sky a condensation of water. And it begins to rain. Torrential storms slowly form oceans in the deep gullies distant from your cliff. As the waters pour from the heavens, they bring with them the chemicals that formed earlier.

This "soup" fills the seas, and also fills the crevices on the land. You see ponds and lakes and oceans; and you see water seeking its own level, thereby forming brooks and streams and rivers.

Some of the smaller pools of fresh water below you are continually filling and then drying by evaporation. You are confused, because you expected life to originate in the sea. But you soon learn that this is not so . . . at least not quite so.

You learn that some of the chemical evolution preceding life is occurring in the lava pools beneath volcanoes; as pools cool, some chemical organization occurs. You also learn that some fresh water ponds, as they evaporate slowly, allow a concentration of those chemicals that will later produce a cell. Without concentration, either in drying ponds or in cooling lava pools, the chemical substances are too dilute; the chance that they will combine in ocean waters is much too slim. But in those ponds that do not dry up completely, you can see the production of some increasingly complicated chemical structures.

Then it begins to rain again, but not as heavily as before. As the "lucky" ponds begin to fill again, their waters overflow and are channeled into the seas; rivers abound. The primeval soup, now with amino acids and other relatively complicated substances—perhaps even some simple living things, you cannot be certain—flows out to sea.

Once at sea, the soup really becomes alive, beyond any doubt. And before your very eyes!

End of story. Rather, a beginning. The beginning.

The story is only a story. It may always remain a story, a theory, a mystery. Where this occurred, and how often it did, are questions most probably never to be answered. But *how* it occurred is open to scientific investigation; at least how it *possibly* could have occurred might be answerable, as we learn more about the geologic past of our planet and about cell and gene chemistry.

We may never ascertain the actual process, but we can learn to (1) assume some logical processes by which chemical evolution yielded life, and (2) rule out others as being chemically or geologically impossible.

How Life Could Have Begun

There is an increasing body of knowledge to help place the theory described above, or modifications of it, on somewhat safe grounds. Experiments of the past two decades have shown that primeval evolution *could* have produced most of the chemical molecules that are essential for the living process.

Starting with the simple chemicals listed in the story above, namely ammonia, water vapor, hydrogen cyanide, and methane, sometimes all of them, sometimes only a few, and exposing them to forces whose existence on the young planet Earth was highly probable—ultraviolet light, heat, electric discharges similar to lightning, radioactivity, and so on—we can convert these to amino acids, the basic building blocks of proteins.

Not only can we form amino acids, but we can combine these into long chains, the proteins. As these chains combine in our test tubes, an easy feat, they form larger particles called *colloids*. Colloid particles soon trap water, to form a surrounding envelope, or shell.

Now, imagine two large drops of water near each

other on a table, and on each drop floats a tiny piece of paper. If you blow on one drop so that it moves and touches the other, then the two drops will merge. You now see, not two small drops but one larger drop of water with two pieces of paper floating thereon. Now that the two pieces of paper are on the same drop, they might stick to each other, whereas they could not before.

Colloids do much the same thing, except that the chemicals therein do not float as did the pieces of paper upon water drops, but are instead trapped inside. If the colloid particles happen to bump into each other, in the test tube, they fuse to form one larger particle with one shell. The combination of several colloid particles in this way is called a *coacervate*.

Coacervates tend to hold on to their water shell more stubbornly than the smaller colloids do. In fact, the water shell is now, because of chemicals now incorporated therein, a membrane rather similar to a cell's outer membrane.

The result of all this chemical organization is a structure, the coacervate, that traps particles from the outside and brings them inside (eats??). This makes it grow, until simple physical forces cause it to split into two smaller coacervate particles (reproduces??).

But it is a long way from a coacervate to a virus, a bacterium, an ameba, or a human liver cell. It is a long way from a coacervate with a shell and an internal chemical factory to a living cell.

The coacervate is certainly not living. And it may never have formed in nature, even if it forms so easily in our laboratories under conditions similar to those in nature. We may be barking up the wrong tree of life.

But we have a working model, a possible model, a start.

Evidence of the Evolution of Animo Acids, Etc.

Let us take a closer look at the laboratory production of chemicals. It is from the following data that some investigators have acquired the idea that there is a logical, chemically possible sequence that leads from ammonia and the other primeval gases to nearly everything that we find in a cell today.

The classic experiment in man-made production of amino acids in a test tube occurred in 1955. Stanley Miller exposed to energy a mixture of the gases we presume to have been present on our young Earth and obtained amino acids. Since then, the experiment has been repeated often, with variation, but with significant results.

Producing a whole protein, however, was another matter. Yet by 1969, a dozen or so small proteins, called polypeptides, had been synthesized in the laboratory, including insulin, simultaneously in the United States and in China. In 1969 also, the first true, larger protein was synthesized; it was one of the cell enzymes that consists of 124 amino acids in a chain. The growth hormone, and several other body hormones, have been produced as well.

Meanwhile, the attention had shifted to the cell's hereditary material, DNA and RNA, called *nucleic acids.* We have already talked about DNA, but not RNA. One type of RNA constitutes the "messenger" mentioned in Chapter IX.

As stated before, nucleic acids are built of basic chemical blocks called nitrogen bases. In 1959, Nobel Prize winner Arthur Kornberg caused a test-tube mixture of chemicals to form new DNA. But his DNA was not biologically normal. On December 14, 1967, however, President Lyndon Johnson told a meeting at the Smithsonian Institution to look to the newspapers the next day for "one of the most important stories you ever read." Dr. Kornberg had now artificially synthesized "normal" DNA molecules, with 5,500 base blocks in each molecule.

RNA, likewise, has been synthesized, first in 1965 at the University of Illinois. Interestingly, in 1968 at Purdue University scientists disassembled a virus, which is a particle made up typically of RNA and coated by protein material; they then reassembled it. Further, they managed to transfer materials from one kind of virus to another kind. Such a transfer could have very far-reaching consequences in human genetic engineering.

Yet, all the above studies on hereditary materials employed, as starting points, materials produced by already living cells or viruses. For this reason, it is very significant that the basic blocks of nucleic acids, A, T, C, and G, can now be manufactured in the laboratory, starting with nitrogen and methane gas. And we can also synthesize simple genetic messages, or "codes."

Not only have cell proteins and nucleic acids—perhaps the two most crucial elements of life—been synthesized. At the University of Wisconsin in 1968, the ribosome— a large structure in cells on which the manufacture of proteins occurs—was artificially synthesized.

Where does all this leave us? Clearly, man has learned to produce the most crucial cell materials and some of the crucial cell parts, and in a very short time. Further, the productions are biologically active; that is, a test tube RNA strand, for example, can multiply itself; in one case, one artificial strand produced 500 billion new strands in fifteen minutes! Man has also learned that once the building blocks are properly assembled, they then can "go it" on their own, because they have properties called self-assembly and self-duplication.

It seems, therefore, that the task of building a cell has been simplified immensely, although the final achievement is still not on the immediate horizon.

Cell Reconstruction

If you disassemble an automobile completely, you no longer have an automobile. The same is true of the living cell; you would no longer have a living cell, but its nonliving parts.

However, by disassembling the automobile you can learn a great deal about its organization, how the parts can be made to work together. Assume, now, that you can reassemble the auto and that it still works. Then you would logically infer that if you could produce the separated parts yourself in your garage, instead of ordering them from Detroit, you could build your own automobile to your own specifications. The same is true of the cell.

The ameba, consisting of three major cell components —the nucleus, the cell lining, or membrane, and everything in between, called the cytoplasm—has been disassembled and then reassembled successfully.

In fact, it is possible to take the membrane of one ameba cell, the cytoplasm of a second, and the nucleus of a third and put them all together to get a normal and functioning ameba cell. In one series of experiments, 80 percent of the reconstituted cells behaved normally. The same thing can be achieved by taking each part from a different strain of ameba. This has not yielded as much success, however, but it has been accomplished. In the series of experiments mentioned above, two fully living and dividing lines of ameba cells were artificially produced, put together from parts of different strains.

Another important tool that assists the biologist in his quest to produce life from nonlife is the use of cell components that are artificially isolated from cells. Certain things in cells continue to work normally, even when they are removed from the cell. For example, from yeast cells we can obtain complete protein-manufacturing systems that function as they would in the cell. This enables us to get a closer look at the process of protein buildup, possibly enabling us to duplicate it in the test tube.

It is also very interesting that DNA, the code, is found in structures other than chromosomes. Some cell structures have their own codes, plus their own protein-manufacturing systems. In brief, it is very nearly true that these structures are self-sufficient, even if normally found in cells.

Based on this discovery of self-sufficient cell structures, the proposal has been advanced that these structures once lived alone, and not in cells; that they once *were* cells, but cells much simpler than most cells known today.

Summary

Man has (1) produced in the laboratory nearly all the chemical substances found in living cells; (2) learned, to some extent, how cells are put together and has himself put some together, but only with parts from already living cells; and (3) devised a scheme to describe how simple chemical substances could have progressively adapted to become so complex as to be called alive, and has proved in the laboratory that this scheme is not impossible.

It is reasonably certain that during the 4 billion years of Earth's history prior to the time when creatures that are now fossils became abundant, a span of time that occupied more than 80 percent of the Earth's existence, *some* process of chemical evolution has occurred. But what the process was is only now beginning to surface. Whatever it was, it was certainly of a much simpler nature than the processes of adaptation seen by man in so short a time span as the last fifty years.

We may be the descendants of bacteria-like cells that lived 3.2 billion years ago, cells able to survive without oxygen, without a well-defined nucleus, without the ability to make their own foods; but cells with a code, a protein-manufacturing system, and the ability to trap foods from their environment.

We might also rejoice that we may not be alone in space. That this same process of chemical evolution is occurring nearby is assumed to be possible. National Aeronautics and Space Administration scientists have for the first time identified amino acids of extraterrestrial origin in a meteorite that fell in Australia in 1969, under conditions that probably preclude contamination from the Earth. The amino acids, five of which are found in living cells, are believed by some to be the first conclusive proof of extraterrestrial chemical evolution.

But regarding our own planet, its life and its test tubes, one might anticipate with anxiety *The New York Times* front page of October 17, 1984, which may read: "Scientists synthesize life at Bethesda, starting with chemicals stored on their shelves. Living cells duplicate, differentiate, and combine into a sponge-like creature that preys, eats, and rests."

And once we can produce cells, then we might reminisce and remember the headline in *Scientific Research* of April 28, 1969: "Tree produced in tissue culture." And this is for real.

A complete test tube tree, an aspen, had formed from separated cells in a test tube garden.

*

THE EARTH:
EXHIBIT A

XII

Earth: Graveyard of Historical Evidence

A bone; a pebble; a shell; markings on mountainsides. Geometry and history in the field. Frozen, fossilized, complete animals are the exceptions. Far more common are the minute, entrenched, broken fragments of past life stored in our Earth's crust, as if for safekeeping.

Discovery of the past is undoubtedly the most difficult and frustrating of human endeavors. Yet it can become the most exciting of achievements, as more and more evidence falls into perspective. To reconstruct an event after it has occurred, and to be reasonably certain that our reconstruction is accurate, demands patience, skill, impartiality, sober reflection . . . and luck. Luck: the correct footstep; the proper turn, the eye darts randomly. To be seen, the bone, the stone, the fossil record must be there of course. Yet even if there, the vestige of ages past may go unnoticed. Luck. Chance. The basic elements of much scientific discovery.

If you have ever witnessed a psychiatrist analyzing a patient's mannerisms or penciled scribbles, a carpenter fingering a doorframe, a dentist glancing at sore gums, you may have experienced pangs of envy. So much evidence can be seen by the expert that is unseen by the novice. A professional sports writer relates a football play; a Broadway critic discounts a musical; so much that is obvious to the trained eye. So it is for the paleontologist.

As he scans the planet for fossils, he sees what remains hidden to most of us. Every feature, every ripple, every elevation, every hint of the past is sought, then explored. The balance of humanity treads by, perhaps never seeing; seldom seeking.

The Crust of History: Shifting Sands

It was explained in Chapter III that the crust of the Earth is in constant motion. Continents move, mountains rise and fall, sea levels rise and fall. Rocks erode. Layers of crusty materials, or of waterborne sediments, pile upon each other to form *strata*.

As each stratum is deposited, it may trap within its substance some life forms, or parts thereof. Stratification is perhaps nowhere as awesome as in the Grand Canyon of Arizona, a section of which is shown in Figure 26. Each stratum represents a span of time past. Generally therefore, but not always, the lowest stratum is the oldest, and the uppermost the youngest. The sedimentation seen on a mountainside (Figure 27) may represent the spanning of millions of years. And the fossil found in a stratum is probably of the same age as the rocks around it.

Figure 26. The Grand Canyon in Arizona, showing stratification.

Earth crust movements can affect climate or soil formation. And climate changes can affect the glaciers and ice
sheets of the Earth. The resulting changes in sea level
can create, or obliterate, land bridges between continents,
and thereby affect migration routes. Many are the ways
by which the changes in the Earth's geology influence the
evolutionary process in the biosphere.

Temperature changes due to geologic events can also
directly affect an animal's ability to survive. If a species
has evolved by adapting to a specific range of temperatures, a temperature that is beyond that range can have
a lethal effect on the species.

It is not surprising that mountain building, or *orogeny*,
is evidenced even today. On February 9, 1971, an earth-

Figure 27. Stratification of sandstone and shale beds near Santa Cruz, California.

quake in the San Gabriel Mountains of California elevated the mountains four inches above the surrounding San Fernando Valley. Evidence suggests that these mountains have risen 12,000 feet in the last 1½ million years. Of related interest is the sliding movement evidenced along the San Andreas geologic fault in California. There is an abrupt difference between the land areas on either side of the fault. The terrain appears to have been cut in a straight line, then one side slid along the other, so that series of hills appear to be artificially separated.

It is believed that every 4 to 5 million years, the topography of the Earth's surface, as well as sea levels, undergoes a marked change. Indeed, our Earth has its own heartbeat, which is constant but irregular.

The Rise and Fall of Glaciers

Imagine the Earth as a distorted sphere, covered with water, with a few specks of crust, land, showing through here and there. It is obvious that as the world temperature lowers, more and more of the water will freeze. Some of the frozen water is over areas called continents; frozen water in these areas produces *ice sheets*, also called continental glaciers, although the latter term is more often reserved for smaller ice sheets. There are today two major ice sheets on the Earth's land: that which covers the Antarctic continent, over the South Pole, and that covering Greenland.

The ice that does not completely cover a continent and the ice that floats upon the oceans constitute *glaciers*.

If environmental temperatures rise, there will be less ice, therefore more water. The water from a melting glacier in the ocean probably does not contribute much to a worldwide rise in sea level, for when a glacier freezes, its ice displaces an equal amount of water; when it melts, the water "takes the place" of the ice again. Also, a melting glacier becomes smaller and lighter, and more of it floats above the water surface; therefore, less water is displaced. The net result is that water from a melting glacier remains in the general vicinity of the glacier and has very little effect in raising the level of the oceans throughout the world.

But if an ice sheet over land and mountainsides melts, then that water necessarily flows away, contributing to a rise in sea level.

Some 15,000 years ago, an ice sheet one mile thick covered the Earth as far south as New York and Oregon. Sea levels were then 400 feet lower than today, and glacier ice covered 27 percent of the Earth's surface, as compared to 10 percent today. It is estimated that if the Antarctic Ice Cap should melt completely, a global rise in sea level of about 100 to 150 feet would result. One might ask what would happen to New York City and to San Francisco.

Since the end of the last ice age, called the "Wisconsin Ice Age" in North America, repeating cycles of warmth and cold have occurred; the world temperature never got low enough to cause massive glaciation, but it sometimes caused slight local ice advances.

Such information is needed by the evolutionist to trace the life forms of the past, to seek the causes for "sudden" proliferation, or extinction, of some species. But how can we determine with some accuracy what past temperatures and sea levels were? There are several methods, some of which I will now discuss.

(1) *Oxygen Isotope Studies.* The atoms which constitute an element, say oxygen, are either stable or unstable atoms. The unstable atoms are said to be radioactive. They release energy in order to become stable; that is, they decay.

The element oxygen has seven such isotopes; i.e., seven different kinds of atoms, four of which are radioactive. The isotope called oxygen-16 is stable, and its atoms constitute 99.76 percent of all the atoms of oxygen. The remaining 0.24 percent consists of atoms of the other six isotopes of oxygen.

It is known that (a) some oxygen is brought down from the skies by precipitation, and (b) the amount of oxygen-18, another isotope of oxygen, in rain or snow depends on the temperature in the area at the time. The lower the temperature, the less oxygen-18 there is in rain or snow. Scientists have dug out a core of ice nearly 9/10 of a mile deep from the Greenland Ice Sheet; in order to determine the climate at various times during the long history of formation of this ice—70,000 to 100,000 years—they simply found the ratio of oxygen-18 to oxygen-16 atoms at different levels of the core. The ratio at any one level is an indication of the local temperature at the time that level froze.

(2) *Peculiarities of Animals*. Some forms of life can survive only within a narrow range of temperatures, as for example one group of the extremely tiny floating sea animals, the foraminifera. If a deep hole is bored into the sediment of the sea floor, and if in a layer we find these forms as fossils, we can then estimate the local temperature at the time that layer of sediment formed.

A second peculiarity of a species that enables us to tell something of its environment at the time it was fossilized is that some water animals can live only in shallow waters. For example, the common edible lobster *Crossostrea virginica* lives in shallow bays usually less than thirteen feet deep. If then we find its fossils much deeper than that in a core dug through the continental shelf, as shown in Figure 28-A, we can be reasonably certain that the water level then was lower than today by a calculable amount. If, on the other hand, fossils of the same species were found above sea level, in a core dug through the dry land, as in Figure 28-B, the sea level at the time it was fossilized could again be determined.

A third, and rather direct tool for climate estimation is a type of foraminifera whose shell is coiled. If grown in cold temperatures, it coils to the left; if in warmth, to the right. Therefore, finding fossils that coil to the right gives an indication that the temperatures at the time were warm. By adding this information to other data from the same area, a more accurate estimate of the temperatures may be obtainable.

(3) *Historical Evidence*. There are areas of the world where slight glacier advances or retreats can have disastrous effects on the lives of people. In this way, western

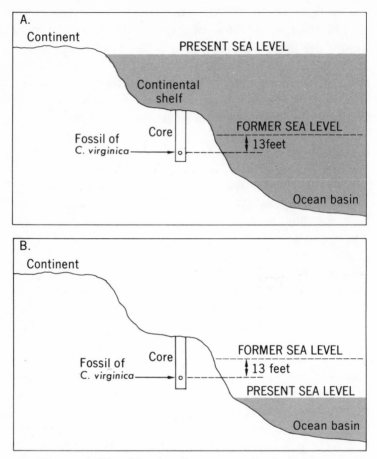

Figure 28. Use of fossil to determine sea levels of the past.

Norway migrations of people provide us with an indication of the times of glacier movements. It is evident that
from 1660 to 1840 A.D. there was a general glacier advance; this led to crop failures, famine, and a drastic
increase in death rate. In Iceland, glaciers retreated from
870 to 1200 A.D., and farms were built, only to be over-
run by advancing ice early in the eighteenth century.

Also, the Viking voyages in the North Atlantic Ocean were partly related to the amount of Arctic Sea ice. The known topography of the Bering Strait, which separates Asia and Alaska, enables us to specify the land that was exposed, surfaced, at different sea levels in the past. This provides historical evidence of those times when migrations would have been possible across the strait. If fossil evidence corroborates the information provided by the above, then the scientist is that much more certain that his theory has some basis of credibility.

There is some evidence that Earth climates are largely influenced by sunspot activity; the greater the heat released from the sun, the hotter is the Earth. So if we obtain records of solar activity, we can get an indication of past Earth climates. There are minor cycles of Earth temperature fluctuations, with ranges of only a few degrees, at 2,500 year intervals; there are also larger fluctuations every 2½ million years. It is the minor cycles that are the ones seemingly related to solar cycles.

For example, the sun was relatively calm from 1645 to 1715 A.D.—the calmest it had been since 300 A.D. This period of calm was followed by sizable glacial advances in Alaska, British Columbia, and Oregon, for example. The severest winters on record from 300 A.D. to the present were in the seventeenth century, during the Little Ice Age. There is therefore an apparent relationship between warm periods and high sunspot activity, and cool periods and times of solar calm.

The next question is if the major temperature shifts— the Ice Ages—have a solar source as well. It cannot be answered at this time.

However, based on the cycles referred to above and on the fact that there have been at least thirty major, and hundreds of minor, oscillations of sea level in the past 600 million years, it is possible to predict that the next major glacial stage could occur 10,000 to 15,000 years from now, as stated before. The next minor, but significant, temperature change could occur around the year 4400.

Fluctuations in sea levels, either from melting ice or from the constant reshaping of the ocean floors, can cause the emergence, or flooding, of vast areas of land; there could easily result mass extinctions. And there have been, as we shall see later.

Imagine the disaster to crops and animal life that can result from the flooding of a local river or stream. Imagine again the impact of a flooded cellar. Imagine how deeply and emotionally affected is man on such a minuscule event as a rainy Monday.

Indeed, life and how it develops and adapts is highly influenced by, and thus reflective of, environmental changes.

And the evidence for many such changes is stored just beneath our feet, in our Earth's crust. It is largely a matter of inventing the proper tools for locating and identifying this evidence that stands in the path of more complete knowledge of the past.

XIII

How Fossils Form and How We Find Them

The processes of orogeny, temperature change, and sea level fluctuations described in the previous chapter are discovered partly by analysis of the fossils stored in the upper crust of our planet, as we have seen.

Fossil science also offers the opportunity to compose a history; the history of the evolution of life on Earth.

A fossil is any evidence of life in the past. It can be a bone, a tooth, shells, footprints, worm trails, tracks, burrows, pollen, dried skin, hair, tendons, dried excrement, or an impression of a part or organ in hardened mud. It can also be a whole organism; an insect trapped in sticky resin flowing from a tree; a mammoth frozen in ice; a mummified carcass. Nearly a quarter of a million fossil insects have been found preserved in amber. In the Rancho La Brea of Los Angeles, organisms have been, and are still being, trapped and fossilized in the sticky tar pools. In

Alaska and Siberia, frozen mammoths have been found nearly intact. The list of fossil finds is extremely long.

However, since most living things, upon death, are immediately attacked by oxygen, or by scavengers such as vultures, bacteria, or a fungus, most soft body parts are never preserved. Ninety-nine percent of known animal fossils are preserved hard parts, such as teeth and bones.

The most common method of fossilization is by rapid burial in a rapidly forming sediment. A typical situation is depicted in Figure 29. Burial in a dust storm, in lava from a volcanic eruption, or quick-freeze trapping can result in protection from scavengers and air.

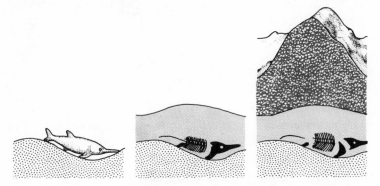

Figure 29. How a buried fossil might remain preserved.

The historic city of Pompeii, a Roman summer resort, was buried on August 24 in 79 A.D. under twenty feet of volcanic ash from Mount Vesuvius, six miles to the north. Impressions of whole families and their domestic animals were preserved as cavities in the ash. In all, 16,000 people died, 80 percent of the city's population. Pompeii "fossils" are not corpses, but casts of corpses. By pouring plastic into the molds, we can produce casts with striking detail of body parts and general structure and form. The bodies had been destroyed by the ravages of time; but the impressions left by those bodies in hardened mud have left behind copies to provide us with horrid, lifelike poses of the panicking citizens.

A series of more valuable finds has been that of the corpses preserved in peat bogs in Denmark. These have been preserved very nearly intact for over 2,000 years! One man, called the Tollund man, was found in 1950. He had died from hanging. His face was strikingly intact, with wrinkles and hair, and a facial expression still very evident. Even the pores of his skin could be seen. Fingernails were intact, and fingerprints could be obtained. In fact, the food he had for his last meal could be determined by examination of the stomach contents—it consisted of a porridge of grain seeds and other plants. This represents a much more valuable find than those of Egyptian mummies; the latter are usually shrunken and dried. The Tollund man was as a man in restful sleep. Indeed, this is fossilization at its best.

At times, when an animal or plant has been trapped, its remains are slowly impregnated, particle by particle, by surrounding minerals. This is called petrification. The result is a petrified fossil, as in the Petrified Forest of Arizona; the fossils sometimes resemble the original structures in exacting detail.

To understand the significance of fossils to evolutionary theory, it must be repeated that when some types of rocks form, they do so in steps—in layers, or strata. The layers are deposited by successive sedimentation from waterborne minerals. Thus, a mountain on land or under water represents a book whose pages tell a story of times past. By deciphering it, the evolutionist may be able to translate the layered evidence into a family tree of life.

Unfortunately, because of the fossilization process itself, the fossil record is rather unsatisfactory. The process preserves mainly those past forms that have become most adapted to their environment. There are few "souvenirs" of transitional, in-between forms, since these did not survive as long and did not therefore produce as many generations as the more adapted species whom they preceded. This is perhaps the main reason why there are the "missing links" at the bottom of Figure 18.

Moreover, the fossil record is biased because the geologic events that have made fossilization most likely have been inconsistent and erratic. They have occurred more often and more profoundly at some times and in some areas than others. We find fossils mainly from certain limited times and within certain limited areas. Further, since soft body parts seldom fossilize, we are often uncertain about the internal anatomies and external features of the forms whose bones we find. Finally, prior to 600 million years ago, when living things probably had no hard parts, fossilization was a rare event; hence there is very little record prior to that time.

Nevertheless, what record has been unearthed has contributed immeasurably to an understanding of evolution. And the fidelity of the record is becoming increasingly verifiable. When the same answer filters through from several different studies by men in varied fields, the likelihood of certainty increases proportionately.

For example, it was mentioned that paleontology contributes to a determination of past geologic events such as climate and sea level changes. Another clue to the past provided by fossil science relates to the number of days in a year, in times past.

It was mentioned in Chapter III that the Earth's spin is possibly slowing down. The twenty-four-hour day is getting longer by two seconds every 100,000 years. Measurements indicate that 500 million years ago an Earth year was 412 days long; 200 million years ago it was 382 days long; 60 million years ago, 371 days long. The year was just as long as it is today—it took the same amount of time for the Earth to complete one revolution around the sun—but a year consisted of more, and shorter, days. A day represents the time it takes for one rotation of the Earth on its own axis. If the spin of the planet is slower now than in the past, then it does not spin as often in a year as it did before.

Now, paleontology has contributed to this theory by discovering as fossils some corals known to have grown in spurts. Their modern relatives have shells that display a thick ring for each year of growth, and a fine line for each day of growth. The modern form of the coral has on the average as many fine lines between thick rings as there are days in a modern year; but fossil forms display an average number of lines that corresponds closely to the number of days per year during their lifetimes, as estimated by other methods. A fossil coral of 400 million years ago shows 398 fine lines per year, on the average.

Finding a Fossil

The secret of success in the use of fossils for building an evolutionary tree depends mainly upon the accurate dating of the stratum in which the fossil was found, or of the fossil itself.

But there is much more. The order of events is usually as follows:

(1) *Find the fossil.* The paleontologist does not merely stroll through the woods at random. He is usually seeking a specific fossil type. He predicts where the find may occur; what was the animal's habitat; what were its food sources; when it lived. If his predictions come true, if he finds something where he thought he would, then he may institute a full-scale search in that area.

(2) *Isolate it.* Quite often a fossil, especially if a hard part, is embedded in rock, and it requires very careful and patient chipping to separate it. It may then be plastered, or otherwise coated, to transfer it to a laboratory for analysis.

(3) *Preserve it.* The fossil may be encased or coated by whatever process will prevent it from deteriorating, now that it has been removed from the coffin that protected it for centuries past.

(4) *Analyze it.* The fossil must now be identified. (a) The animal or plant of which it was a part is determined; (b) the missing parts of the organism are reconstructed, if possible; (c) the relationship of the organism to other fossil finds is assessed; (d) the fossil is dated—how old is it?

The trained paleontologist can often identify an animal by a single tooth, a thigh bone, a lower jaw, a foot print. To reconstruct, he may begin by locating the regions of a bone where muscles were attached; a permanent mark often may remain at that point. From the size and geometry of the bone, and of associated bones if found, he may be able to determine how thick and long a muscle needed to be to lift the bone. Piece by piece, fossil by fossil, a complete framework may be built. Leverage principles, preserved skin fragments or impressions, and anatomical laws all assist his reconstruction of the past.

Specialized techniques have added not only to fossil analysis, but to discovery as well. Paleontologists have begun to use the electron microscope, with its extremely powerful magnification, and the exposure of rocks to infrared or to ultraviolet light. By the use of such measures, some features not seen easily by the unaided eye become more visible. X rays are sometimes used to determine the atomic makeup of fossil parts, such as the bones of domesticated animals already mentioned.

Indeed, paleontology is rapidly becoming a highly specialized science that takes advantage of the instrumentation developed by the other sciences.

Dating a Fossil

It is perhaps the first consideration of the paleontologist who "gets a bite" to know how old his discovery is; where it fits into the family tree of the evolving biosphere.

It was mentioned earlier, with reference to oxygen, that some isotopes—some kinds of atoms—of an element are stable, and some are not. In order to stabilize, the unstable atoms decay at a constant and measurable rate.

Now, although a block of any element will usually have both stable and unstable atoms, imagine a block of atoms, all identical, all radioactive. You would find that you cannot predict when ony one specific atom before you will decay, but that you can predict with great accuracy how long it will take for one-half of the unstable atoms to decay. This time is called the *half-life* of that isotope.

For any one isotope, the half-life is a universal constant; i.e., the rate of decay has always been the same. Some isotopes have half-lives in the order of seconds, others in the order of billions of years. But the fact that scientists can determine the half-life accurately has permitted the paleontologist to use some radioisotopes as reliable "clocks." Some such radioisotope clocks are considered to be 98 percent accurate. Let us survey one method.

One stable isotope of carbon is carbon-12; we will write it C-12, although it is conventional to write ^{12}C. An unstable atom of carbon is carbon-14. In the Earth's atmosphere, there is a gas called carbon dioxide, already referred to and written as CO_2, which green plants trap and utilize to make carbohydrates and other foods. That is why animals depend ultimately on plants for survival; animals cannot make foods; plants can.

When a plant leaf traps CO_2, most of the carbon in it is C-12, since C-12 constitutes nearly 99 percent of all carbon atoms. But a small amount, about 1 percent, of the carbon in the trapped CO_2 is carbon-14.

This is how you would date a fossil by the carbon-14 method: the ratio of C-12 to C-14 in the atmosphere is assumed to be constant; let us call this ratio 99 to 1. Therefore, when a plant traps these two isotopes, out of every 100 carbon atoms, 99 will be C-12 and 1 will be C-14.

When the plant incorporates the carbon atoms into foods and into plant tissues, then again the foods and tissues will have 99 C-12 atoms for every 1 C-14 atom. And the ratio is maintained when carbon passes from plant to animal, as when the rabbit eats the carrot; it is also maintained when the fox eats the rabbit.

Now, when a plant or animal dies, no more carbon enters that organism for it no longer eats or traps CO_2—it is dead. But since the C-14 in the corpse continues to decay, being radioactive, then the ratio of C-12 to C-14 changes, and does so at a constant rate.

To date the fossil by this method, one merely finds the ratio of these two isotopes of carbon in the fossil; the older the find, the less carbon-14 remains. The accuracy of this method is limited to 50,000 years; beyond that there is so little carbon-14 left that our instruments are incapable of detecting it, or of measuring it with accuracy.

Several other methods of dating have been applied, some with greater reliability than others: tree-ring analysis, estimates of sedimentation or erosion rates, fluorine content method (the more fluorine, the older the fossil), nitrogen content method (the less nitrogen, the older the fossil), and other radioisotope methods (uranium-238, thorium-230, protactinium-230, lead-206, potassium-40, etc.).

In order to use many of these methods with accuracy, it is essential that a fossil be so resistant to change that it remained relatively intact from the time it fossilized.

Because such a permanent record of life is filed within our Earth's crust, the paleontologist can reconstruct a history of the past. The finding, dating, and identifying of fossils can help to form a framework upon which to build a time scale of biological history.

XIV

A Time Scale. We Need a Time Scale

One man, Charles Lyell (1797–1875), almost single-handedly established the concept called uniformitarianism. It implied that the Earth undergoes gradual and constant change, and development. Lyell's theory was very influential in overturning many previous concepts, especially those related to the age of the Earth. Many estimates had been made, some based on Biblical passages. In the seventeenth century, for example, Christian scholars believed that the Earth was 6,000 years old. But Lyell's theory led to a concept of unlimited time, a new concept to many.

From 1860 to 1909, estimates of the age of the Earth ranged from 3 million to 1,584 million years, based mostly on estimates of the rates of rock formation.

But Lyell's theory was somewhat too strict. There is gradual change, but it is not "uniform"; there are times

Figure 30. The timetable of Earth history.

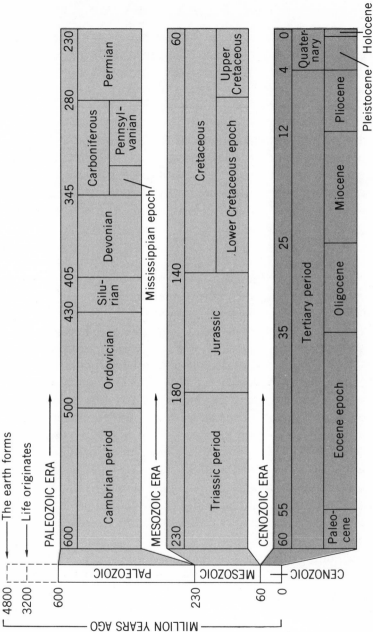

when changes are abrupt, as we have seen concerning orogeny, climate shifts, and changes in sea levels.

Based on the fossil record as it developed after Lyell's time, and on the recent dating of rocks with accuracy, a timetable was devised, and is shown in Figure 30. It is being revised constantly, as new information becomes available. The time boundaries were shifted often during the early days of paleontology, but are only slightly changed now. These boundaries represent times of drastic and abrupt changes in the history of the Earth and/or of its life forms. A boundary may represent a sudden temperature change, a sudden appearance of a fossil, or its sudden disappearance.

Notice in Figure 30 that the three major eras, Paleozoic, Mesozoic, and Cenozoic, are represented to scale vertically on the left, but are expanded horizontally, going to the right, each era being expanded to a different time scale in the figure. The entire Cenozoic era (bottom), for example, is equal in time to the Devonian period (top).

The geologic timetable, which perhaps should now be called the geobiologic timetable, since so much of it is based on biologic events—indeed, it may futuristically be called the ecologic timetable—begins at 600 million years ago, and for a good reason. Very few fossils are found that are older than 600 million years. Although life probably originated nearly 3 billion years ago, life forms prior to 600 million years ago probably lacked hard parts, as already mentioned. Secondly, many Precambrian rocks later reformed, possibly destroying most fossils therein, if any.

Figure 31 depicts the times when the main and dominant life forms inhabited the Earth, during the Paleozoic

Figure 31. Outline of major events during Paleozoic and Mesozoic eras.

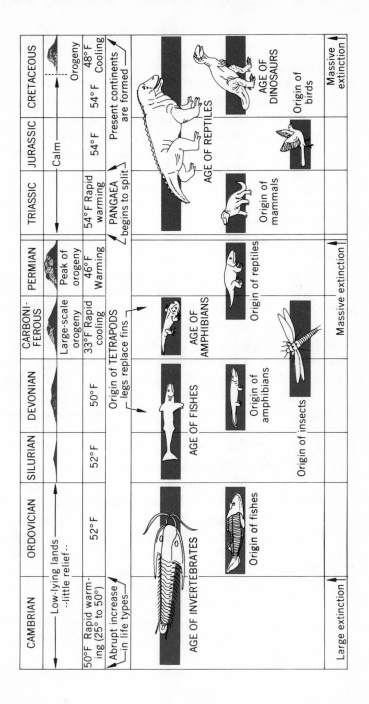

CAMBRIAN	ORDOVICIAN	SILURIAN	DEVONIAN	CARBONI-FEROUS	PERMIAN	TRIASSIC	JURASSIC	CRETACEOUS
Low-lying lands --little relief--				Large-scale orogeny	Peak of orogeny	Rapid warming	Calm	Orogeny
50°F Rapid warming (25° to 50°)	52°F	52°F	50°F	33°F Rapid cooling	46°F Warming	54°F Rapid warming	54°F	54°F → 48°F Cooling
Abrupt increase in life types			Origin of TETRAPODS — legs replace fins			PANGAEA begins to split	Present continents are formed	
AGE OF INVERTEBRATES	Origin of fishes	AGE OF FISHES		AGE OF AMPHIBIANS	Origin of reptiles	AGE OF REPTILES		AGE OF DINOSAURS
			Origin of amphibians			Origin of mammals		Origin of birds
		Origin of insects						
Large extinction				Massive extinction				Massive extinction

and Mesozoic eras. The Cenozoic era will be the subject
of later chapters. The times of rapid mass extinctions, due
to flooding, temperature changes, drying, and so on, are
also shown, as are some major events of Continental Drift.
It is interesting that so much of the evolution of life occurred while the Earth's land surface was still concentrated
on one massive continent.

In Figure 31, the times when life forms flourished and
dominated the biosphere are labeled "The Age of . . . ." To
qualify as a dominant form, a species or larger category
of animals or plants have to have been the forms best
adapted to the environment, thereby becoming the ones
with the greatest impact on the biosphere around them.

Notice in the figure that although some groups may
have originated at certain times, it took perhaps millions
of years before they could dominate. Charles Darwin of-
fered this principle: survival of the unspecialized. It implies that as a species becomes more and more well
adapted to its environment, it comes to master that environment; yet if the environment changes, then generally
the forms not perfectly adapted to the old environment
are the ones which can adapt most easily to the new one.
This is certainly true in our own lives, as it seems to be
true in the lives of plants and animals.

In concluding this chapter, let us remember one thing:
not all animal and plant phyla have come to dominate the
world. Most did not. The inability to dominate is not necessarily related to the inability to survive. For example,
mammals survived quite adequately for over 150 million
years, from the Triassic period to the beginning of the
Cenozoic era, before they dominated the land.

XV

The Dinosaurs: Were They Really Overspecialized?

Imagine the following scene.

You are standing on the edge of an endless swamp. There are few noises to hear. Leaves rustling, insects chirping, animals treading; but you are the only person on Earth. No roads, no houses, no telephone cables, no conversation, no tools. Merely animals walking, screaming, socializing, preying.

To your right there appears a long-necked monster you have never seen before. Man will later find his fossilized bones; he will strain to understand why the monster became extinct. Within the shallow waters of a distant pond you see the bulky frame of an even larger dinosaur shredding a small tree. It must weigh 100 tons!

Fascinating cooperation is evident everywhere. Plants abound, dinosaurs abound, strange-looking "birds" roam the skies above you. Merciless hunting abounds, yet everyone stops short of species destruction. They hunt, but they are not hunting to destroy; merely to eat. All is calm; all is adapted; the climate is tropical and has been for at least a million years.

Suddenly, your time-lapse brain, viewing long stretches of time as if they were constricted to but a moment, hears the crackling of Earth. You turn to see a slow and gradual upwelling from the ground. Mountains are forming! The Earth offers a panoramic view of orogeny; fascinating, but frightening. The Earth undulates beneath your feet.

Then you feel a chill. It is cooling. The waters around you are receding, as if sucked away by nature. The calm is gone. Wilting plants; huge bulks of walking life collapsing before you; starvation. Gradually, other massive forms drop. Starvation. Eaten by scavengers, tiny little scavengers rushing out of their hiding places for a free and rare treat. A gigantic wake for forms long dominant; a wake attended by the next in line, thousands of timid mammals long suppressed into trunks and burrows and caves.

You are witnessing the extinction of the dinosaurs!

The next instant, you see a rapid increase in the numbers of the small mammals; now free to roam, to prey, to adapt, to evolve. Mammals: long ago derived from early reptiles, held in abeyance, now finally becoming the ruling class, as they grow in size, in numbers, in intelligence.

Such was the history of life at the end of the Mesozoic era. The picture is possibly not as accurate as the story appears; there are varying theories. But a picture there was, and we have witnessed how it could have appeared. A few feet of water no longer there, resulting in the massive extinctions you witnessed. Evolution jumping another step; the sudden change in environment causing a sudden emergency. What an impact can a minor change have on life and genes so well adapted.

The dinosaur dynasty offers by far the most intriguing of evolutionary events. Animals gifted with large pituitary glands that released vast amounts of growth hormones, but not gifted with intelligence; animals ruling by bulk.

It is erroneous to say that the dinosaurs, one of seven different types of reptiles, were unsuccessful organisms. Any group that lived for as long as they did certainly deserves the title of successful. On a scale of 365 days, to represent the time since the Cambrian period, they lived for 70 days, while man has lived only for one day. If man lives another 50 million years, he will have existed less than half as long as did the dinosaurs.

Nor were they overspecialized. They were specialized adequately, enough to rule the life around them for over a hundred million years!

Reptiles vs Mammals

Dinosaur and man. Reptile and mammal. What really differentiates one from the other? Obviously, if we compare advanced reptiles and advanced mammals, such as dinosaurs and men, the differences are many. But if we view the *stem*, the early reptiles which gave rise to mammals, then we find very little difference between early reptiles and early mammals. Such fossils are difficult to classify as one or the other.

As is true in so many other transition stages, such as between life and nonlife, matter and energy, simple plant and simple animal, we must be arbitrary. We must apply arbitrary definitions.

In this case, paleontologists who classify vertebrate

skeletons have selected this one criterion: a fossil skeleton belongs to the class *Reptilia* if two small bones of the lower jaw have not become ("have not evolutionarily moved up to . . .") two of the small inner ear bones. If they have, if a fossil has these two bones in its ear region instead of at the lower jaw, it is of the class *Mammalia*.

It is worth noting that if you had been present when the first mammal evolved from reptiles, you would not have called the new form a mammal, but a reptile with something wrong; with an abnormality in bone positioning. Only after centuries would it have become obvious that this new form was indeed becoming a different kind of vertebrate, to persist to become more and more different from the stem from whence it came.

But with the end of the reptile dynasty we now come to the origin of man. Before we leave, however, let us appreciate the fact that there are, for all of us to see: the awe-inspiring dinosaur tracks, the bones of grotesque bulks reaching out to museum ceilings, and the models of these giants of survival sprinkled across state parks.

Perhaps it should give man pride in his fascinating brain to realize that nature has finally selected for intelligence, and not bulk.

*

MAN THE PROSECUTOR

XVI

Man: The Brainchild of Evolution

Man. Who is he? Who is this creature so intellectually superior to all other inhabitants of the biosphere?

Is he the culmination of the evolutionary process? Or is he merely another member of the cave generation; a stem man; a pre-man? Is he to become known as the primitive missing link between the caveman and the populations of future centuries?

He is certainly still animalistic, as we stated earlier. He is very emotional, largely controlled by hormones, often tending to mass hysteria, highly conscious of territorial boundaries, and not at all well adapted to the bacteria and viruses that do him harm. He is aggressive, often instinctively; he can become a twentieth-century cannibal for purposes of nationalistic or personal reputation or economy. He establishes a class order, a dominance hierarchy which has its parallels in other animals. He is highly influenced by his genes and his surroundings. He has fears and desires often insurmountable. And, as other advanced animals, his society depends in a fragile way upon the establishment of social bonds; bonds which he needs sometimes as much as he needs food. And overpopulation or underpopulation, crowding or loneliness, can threaten these bonds; can kill him.

But if we look carefully, we see that man can overcome the powerful natural forces constantly tugging at his mind, and thereby display the significant extra which he has extracted from the evolutionary process. He displays what is his, and his alone: an awesome, uniquely human, and extremely complex interweaving of mental powers. Natural selection has selected a brain so capable, so elusive, so adaptive, that man is indeed the biological culmination of a natural process billions of years old. He is indeed able to produce and direct future evolution, not only of his plants and animals, but of himself as well. Three million nerve cells send information to his central nervous system, but only 350,000 bring information back; what occurs in between is the greatest achievement of evolution. This is why some refer to the Holocene period as the psychozoic age, the age of awareness.

"And all this from monkeys?"

No!

Man did not evolve from monkeys. But then, who were his ancestors? Where did man come from? How were his ancestors influenced to yield *Homo sapiens sapiens*?

Man. An erect, highly intelligent, domineering two-legged animal with stereoscopic vision, whose body is still 75 percent water, whose genes contain small fragments of an unbroken line of protoplasm stemming back millions of years. No. He did not evolve from monkeys. He evolved from the same source that monkeys did, from the same stem. Monkey and man are both contemporaries; their common ancestor is dead.

Let us attempt to catalogue ourselves.

Man the Mammal

The mammals, we have already seen, arose during the Mesozoic era, but did not achieve dominance until the Cenozoic. The latter geologic period is appropriately termed the Age of Mammals.

The original ancestors of man, to start at an arbitrary point, lived in water. They were not mammals, but fish. But during the late Paleozoic and the Triassic, there were seasonal droughts which must have affected water-dependent species drastically, mainly by reducing the amount of available oxygen in the waters. It appears obvious, from the fossil record, that these forms gradually evolved a lunglike structure that enabled them to gulp air directly above the surface of the shallow waters, instead of depending on gills to absorb oxygen directly from the water. In fact, it has been found that the majority of late Paleozoic freshwater fish had such lunglike structures, similar to those in modern lungfish.

If you are unable to imagine a fish with lungs, picture the confusion of a twenty-second-century boy gaping at a photograph of a propeller-driven airplane.

Once some animal structures, functions, or behaviors became advantageous outside water, the stage was set for more and more such adaptations.

Fins experienced strong selection pressure if by chance they mutated even slightly to favor their use in pushing the animal forward, in a crawling motion near the banks of shallow waters, instead of propelling it forward as in an aquatic medium. This was a prelude to walking. Examples of such mutations could be a more muscular fin, or a fin cut into sections.

The modified fish could then move from stream to stream in periods of drought. Slowly, gradually, these fish types evolved into organisms with limbs, as is amply demonstrated again by the fossil record.

At first, limbs were bulky and barely manageable, but nevertheless they allowed their owners to move on land. This was obviously more advantageous to an animal than merely being able to wade near the surface of the pond, gulping air, as the lunged fish did. Thus it was that limbs proliferated, and that amphibians arose.

Yet even these "new" animals had to return to water to copulate and to lay their eggs. Their early life was spent in water, as is true of modern amphibians. Even as adults they were more comfortable in water, as are modern frogs, since their lungs were not yet as efficient in capturing oxygen from the air as was their skin in capturing it from water.

Thus it was that fish invaded the land, 350 million years ago. It took almost 100 million years before amphibians achieved their own status, becoming the dominant forms of life.

Some of the animals that could venture onto dry land eventually evolved an egg that could survive on land. There resulted a strong selection pressure for such an adaptation, since land eggs were much less likely to be devoured by predators, especially since most sizable animals at that time were bound to the waters. The land egg was self-sufficient, with yolk for a food reserve, and a hard shell. This was coupled with a slowly evolved adaptation to reproducing on land, wherein sperm must be deposited into the female animal, instead of simply being released in water.

The combination of internal fertilization and the land egg gave rise to a new category of vertebrate animals called the reptiles.

After a time, there arose small reptiles with mammalian features, named the therapsids, or mammal-like reptiles. In the Triassic, therapsids came very close to mammal status, with a mammal-like skeleton, *except* for the two bones of the lower jaw, as explained before. So we arbitrarily call them reptiles, mammal-like reptiles.

Perhaps the most significant change which occurred, while reptiles were slowly acquiring what we now call mammalian traits, was an increase in body activity. This necessitated changes in blood circulation patterns and various other changes in internal mechanisms, including a shift from coldbloodedness to warmbloodedness. There was also a need for a greater exchange of gases by breathing. To assist this need, a dome-shaped muscle, the *diaphragm,* evolved to span the inside of the chest completely, thereby separating the torso into a thorax and an abdomen. This greatly increased the efficiency of breathing. Further, the red blood cells, carriers of oxygen, lost their nucleus, enabling them to carry more oxygen. "Lost their nucleus," in an evolutionary sense, means that natural selection selected for those animals least likely to succumb and die when faced with the need for greater oxygen uptake.

Therefore, there survived more of those animals *able* to maintain a high degree of activity.

In addition to altered red blood cells, a diaphragm, and warmbloodedness, the hemoglobin (oxygen-carrying chemical substance) in the red blood cells evolved to "catch" more and more oxygen, so that eventually mammal hemoglobin attained an oxygen-carrying capacity three times that of reptiles.

Finally, mammals evolved also the ability to carry the young inside the mother's womb, for a relatively long time. This enabled the body to produce the organs and nervous system necessary to cope with the environment more adequately when it was born.

These innovations, some seemingly minor perhaps,

made "all the difference in the world" in survival ability. But the mammals that first evolved were nevertheless suppressed for millions of years, mainly due to the dominance of dinosaurs. This is why they remained quite small. The Eocene horse was as small as a pig, and so were ancestors of the elephant 50 million years ago.

We may now summarize the traits of mammals, as well as add others, to indicate why the taxonomist places an animal in the class *mammal*.

(1) A womb, at least in some mammals, that harbors and supports the embryo;

(2) mammary (milk) glands that supply nutrition to the newborn;

(3) temperature-regulating devices, maintaining a constant internal temperature—warmbloodedness;

(4) body hair, that acts as insulation against external changes in temperature, for example;

(5) altered red blood cells with hemoglobin that has a greater attraction for oxygen;

(6) a diaphragm that improves the breathing process;

(7) a four-chambered heart that improves circulation.

Man the Primate

Let us now review the basis for taxonomic classification of man as a member of the order *primates*. In order to realize why primates have the traits listed, we must first know the environmental factors that predominated at the time of primate evolution, in the early Cenozoic era.

By the end of the Paleozoic era, flowering plants had begun to evolve, and by 120 million years ago they had become distributed throughout the warmer regions of the Earth. As a result, during the early Cenozoic there occurred the simultaneous evolution of the many kinds of plants in tropical forests, and of the mammal groups living in these forests. The mammals we are interested in here are those belonging to the primate order.

The first primates that evolved are called prosimians, and are today represented by three living groups, the lemurs, the shrews, and the tarsiers. As primates took to the trees, the habitat that provided the most food, they became more and more adapted to an arboreal life. Living in trees, searching the ground and other trees for prey, jumping from branch to branch, obviously imposed a very new set of demands upon structure, function, and behavior.

Through the 5 million years of the Paleocene epoch, the traits listed below adapted the primates to an arboreal habitat.

   (1) Manual grasping:
      (a) flat nails replacing claws;
      (b) longer digits for a stronger grasp;
      (c) an opposing thumb. If all five digits are on one plane, as when your hand is lying flat on a table, and your thumb is pressed against the other fingers, you may find it difficult to grasp a pencil if you do not move your thumb away. However, by being able to move the thumb to the opposite side of the pencil, as if making a fist, the problem can be solved easily.
      (d) Prehensile fingers and toes; that is, digits flexible and jointed enough to wrap around a branch;
      (e) increase in sensitivity of the sense of touch, mainly at the fingertips and in the hairless palm.
   (2) Improved vision:
      (a) orbits, the bony cavities in which lie the eyeballs, are in the front of the face, instead of at

the sides as in most other vertebrate animals. A three-dimensional perspective is very helpful in moving from branch to branch. If you close one eye and attempt to hit a baseball, or drive a car, you may experience difficulty in determining how far an object is, and how thick or deep it is.

(b) the bony orbit is completely encased, except in front of course, and protected by the bony and bulky protruding eyebrow ridges.

(c) Color vision.

(3) Social organization:

(a) Social bonds: primates have evolved behavioral patterns whereby they can make themselves known in their band or family. Such bonds help in cultural exchange, and in the pooling of resources, all of which are advantageous for more efficient hunting, trapping, territorial maintenance, protection from predators, etc. The major impetus to increased socialization was probably the constant quest for food. Whatever traits enabled a population to better assure a constant food supply have been selected in favor of other traits. Social bonage is one such trait.

(b) Social behavior: to *maintain* the social bonds, primates have evolved various behaviors; a dominance hierarchy often called a pecking order (wherein males especially are genetically predetermined, to lead in varying degrees), gregariousness, territoriality, parental care, mother-child recognition, social play, social communication, and so on. Many such behaviors are crucial, not only to a group on a hunting mission, but also for the transmission of acquired knowledge from one generation to the next.

(c) Comparative longevity: any modification that enables a generation to pass on more culture, more of its acquired knowledge, to its off-spring obviously experiences strong selection pressure. The longer the life span of primate parents, the longer they are able to protect and to teach the young.

(d) Prolonged infancy: the longer an offspring stays with its parents, the more it can learn, hence the less chance that its later predator-prey contacts will be resolved only by trial and error. If it knows how to hunt and how to protect itself *before* it needs to do so, then when its time comes it will be more likely to survive. In the past therefore, those primates genetically prone to stay-at-home survived more often than those more likely to elope. Stay-at-home genes then were passed on more often than elope genes. Of course, the causes of staying at home or of eloping are not re-stricted to genes. But they are affected *in part* by heredity, therefore are subjected *in part* to the forces of natural selection.

It is possible that the rough play of young boys, whereby they appear very aggressive, but most often stop short of really hurting "the enemy," is a remnant of such social play in simpler primates than man, whereby the young males learned the motions of fighting at home, before leaving to face the real thing. Interestingly, we see much less of this in young girls, whose role, at least until the present century, has been the subordinate role of the mother caring for the home and children.

(e) Tendency to single births: this primate trait is an outcome of an arboreal life, where it is simpler to protect and feed few offspring rather than many. Resulting from this has been the reduction of milk glands to two, compared to the many glands of other mammals, such as cats and dogs.

Therefore, by adapting to the tropical forests abounding in the early Cenozoic, small, shrewlike primates—some three inches long, with poor eyesight—gave rise to larger primates with frontal eyes, an improved sense of balance and touch, and limbs for climbing and for swinging from branch to branch.

Such forelimb swinging from branch to branch, which increases the animal's speed tremendously, is called *brachiation*. The modern expert brachiator is the gibbon.

Resulting from a shift to brachiation were the following traits: (1) the shift from horizontal to upright posture; (2) emancipation of the forelimbs, allowing them to be used for other purposes, such as probing, carrying, reaching out to other branches, and feeding; and (3) the transfer of these functions from the mouth to the forelimbs, freeing the mouth for the development of *speech*.

Man the Hominid

Besides being a mammal and a primate, man is also an anthropoid, a hominoid, and a hominid, as we saw previously.

Let us note some of the traits that enable us to classify man as a hominid.

(1) An increasingly erect posture.

(2) Marked reduction of canine and molar teeth. What the canines did previously, for example grasping into a prey, now could be done by the hands.

(3) Gradual loss of the opposability of the big toe. When some primates left the trees, as we will see in the next chapter, and reassumed a life on land, the hind limb that was once adapted to grasping branches now became adapted to supporting the animal upright, on the ground. There was no longer a need for an opposable big toe.

Man is the only surviving hominid. Earlier hominids, which we will call pre-men, included the members of the genus *Australopithecus,* one member of whom we will meet in Chapter XIX. More recent members of our ancestry included *Homo erectus* and the Neanderthal man, whom we will also meet.

Man the Homo sapiens sapiens

Now that we have catalogued man as a mammal, a primate, and a hominid, let us see what differentiates him from all other hominids of the past:

(1) Completely upright posture and nearly perfected two-legged locomotion.

(2) Unlike the apes and most other primates, the legs are much longer than the arms.

(3) A very large brain, especially anteriorly, providing a greater intellect and greater ability to learn.

(4) A vertical face. There is less jutting out of the jaws than in many apes and pre-men, and an enlargement forward of part of the skull to accommodate the forebrain.

(5) Canine teeth about the same size as the others, since their original function has become lost.

(6) Considerable reduction of eyebrow ridges; skulls of apes and pre-men display large brow ridges protecting eyes and assisting in use of jaws.

(7) The point where the skull pivots upon the spine is nearer the center of the skull base; this supports the skull better since it is nearer its center of gravity.

Since there have existed other forms of *Homo sapiens* in the past such as Neanderthal man, called *Homo sapiens neanderthalensis,* modern man is given a slightly different name, to differentiate him from the others: *Homo sapiens sapiens.*

Homo sapiens sapiens arose with the advent of Cro-Magnon man 40,000 years ago. In referring to man from that time on, we need not use the second *sapiens* in his name, since there now exists only one subspecies of *Homo sapiens,* and that is the form now dominating the Earth.

XVII

The Weather
and How It Brought Us Home

In the previous chapter, we placed the ancestors of man up in the trees and surveyed the adaptations that resulted from that habitat.

In this chapter we will bring pre-man down from the trees.

Forests with Receding Tree Lines—New Kinds of Apes

By the end of the Oligocene epoch, 25 million years ago, the monkeys and primitive apes had evolved. A significant climatic change during the Miocene caused the selection for bipedalism and the subsequent evolution of pre-men.

But as the Cenozoic era proceeded, there occurred periodic onsets of drought, and this imposed serious demands upon the forest community in which primate evolution had thus far occurred. Nature then began to select for smaller plants; plants not so dependent on heavy rainfall. This led to the death of many tropical plants.

There resulted, in many localities, low grassland communities called "savannas," such as is shown in Figure 32.

Figure 32. A water hole at Amboseli: early man lived on such savannas.

As the heavily camouflaged and moist habitat gave way to open fields with only occasional clusters of trees, there must have resulted a fierce competition for shelter and food. The survivors of this battle must have been either those best adapted to tree living, or those least dependent on such a life and able to leave the forest and survive on the open grounds. This led to a polarization of primates into tree primates and ground primates. Figure 33 outlines some of the major Cenozoic events listed thus far.

The grasslands, as evidenced from fossil finds from

Figure 33. Outline of major events during Cenozoic era.

Million years ago

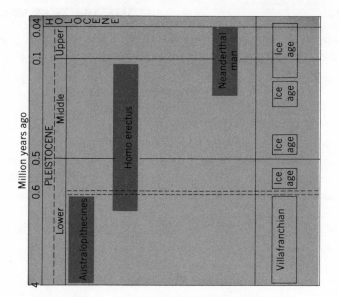

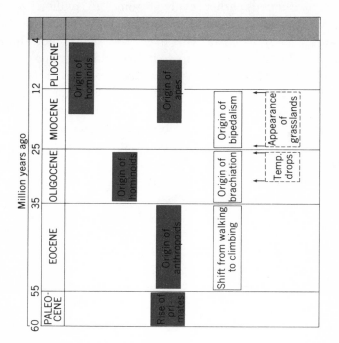

such areas, slowly became the new home of some primates, those that subsequently gave rise to man.

Again the Need to Change

What might have been some adaptations selected at this
time? Socialization was now increasingly advantageous.
So were height, speed, and increased intelligence, par-
ticularly improved memory and foresight, all to assist in
the hunt.

Food seems to have been the most powerful and consistent natural selector. Many of the adaptations of pre-
man seem to have occurred in answer to this need.

As the Miocene proceeded, some forms of primates
became specialists in bipedalism. The brachiating anatomy mentioned earlier evolved some 10 million years
sooner in the Oligocene. It was now simplifying into the
anatomy of bipedalism. However, you should not think
that brachiation evolved *so that* it could later make bipedalism possible. Brachiation evolved because of its own
survival value at the time. Then, much later and only in
some animals, it was replaced by bipedalism, because this
trait now had survival value for these animals.

When some anthropoids, mainly the heavier ones, left
the trees, some 40 million years after early primates had
originally begun to climb trees, several behavioral changes
ensued. For example, they became much more aggressive,
and still are, as evidenced by comparing modern arboreal
primates to terrestrial ones. Maintaining a grassland territory is much more difficult than maintaining a forest
territory.

It was at this time that hominoids diverged into the
apes and the pre-men. The gibbon and simian apes, both

relatively lightweight organisms, have remained arboreal; all other apes and pre-men left the trees.

Possibly the first pre-man was *Ramapithecus*. Some anthropologists, who study the origin of man and his development, disagree. This fellow appeared 15 million years ago, possibly derived from a group of ground apes called *Proconsul*, whom you will meet in Chapter XIX. *Ramapithecus* had a dentition more manlike than apelike. On the other hand, *Proconsul* was definitely an ape. And the fellow that possibly evolved from *Ramapithecus*, namely *Australopithecus africanus*, was more manlike than apelike.

Therefore, we call *Proconsul* an ape, *Ramapithecus* a man-ape, and *Australopithecus* an ape-man. It is not until the appearance of the genus *Homo* that we use the un-qualified term "man."

Ramapithecus probably used his forelimbs for defense or food-gathering. Some evidence suggests that he may have been a rock thrower; if true, this would indicate the first use of objects external to the primate body to achieve a definite and planned function.

During the Pliocene there probably occurred, in the terrestrial forms, a further refinement of bipedal anatomy and of socialization, less emphasis on vision, and selection for bulk and speed. Then, at the end of the Pliocene, severe geologic events and climate changes caused the appearance and distribution of radically new traits, mainly behavioral.

The Hunt

A time of calm marked the onset of the Pleistocene, and this time lasted until the first of four Pleistocene Ice Ages.

In Figure 33, most of the Lower Pleistocene, prior to 600,000 years ago, is compressed on the scale, whereas the time span from 600,000 years ago to the present has been expanded to show the times of some major events. The probable range of time when some of our ancestors lived, as deduced from the fossil record, is indicated, as is also the probable duration of each Ice Age.

Planned hunting seems to have originated during the lower Pleistocene. Since a planned hunt, where a site is preselected and a group leaves in unison as do human week-enders on their way to the woods, is generally more efficient than a random hunt by one or two individuals, there was strong selection pressure for planning, hence for improved memory and foresight. In an evolutionary sense therefore, the best thing that could have happened to bring man on the scene, retroactively thinking, was the Oligocene-Miocene climate shift that caused some apes to leave the forests. In a very real sense, hunting induced nature to seek and favor the traits that led to that species called *Homo sapiens.*

The hunting process led to such a rapid increase in brain size that during the rise of hunting the brain nearly doubled in volume.

Coincidentally with an increase in brain size there occurred:

(1) A need for a larger female pelvis to allow the birth of this larger brained pre-human. To understand how the human pelvis supports the internal organs, and how it had to evolve to be able to expand to allow the process of childbirth, cup your hands as if to carry as much water as you can in them. Then, as if to let fall only some of the water, open the bottom of the cup; this is what happens in the birth process.

(2) The anatomical changes required of the female

pelvis, however, would have tended to reduce the running speed of women. Probably to compensate for this, nature evolved a shorter gestation period, so that the infant would be born before the brain became too large to pass through the birth canal. This allowed the evolutionarily developing female to retain some speed, yet allowed the child to remain in the protective womb until biologically better able to face the world.

(3) Because the baby was born sooner, an adaptation that favored the mother, there resulted a selection for a longer infancy period, partly to make up for time lost from the womb. This can be seen by comparing the duration of relative "helplessness" of infants of different kinds of anthropoids: monkeys are helpless for a year after birth, apes for two to three years, *Homo erectus* (known only as fossils) for four to five years, and modern man for six to eight years. This proposes a second purpose for a long infancy, namely continued biological development, beyond that previously mentioned, the transmission of knowledge and culture.

(4) It is further possible that the slower running speed of females may have been one of the contributing factors to a family structure, where the female remained at home and hunting became relegated to the increasingly faster and stronger male.

Another shift in hunting practices, this time from hunting small animals to hunting big game, which occurred 2 million years ago, must also have led to a rapid increase in brain size, as the fossil record seems to indicate. This shift was probably undertaken by *Australopithecus africanus,* and eventually led to the first member of the genus of man, *Homo erectus.*

Now, it is interesting that the human brain continued

its rapid increase in size until 50,000 to 100,000 years ago, then ceased growing. This implies that Upper Pleistocene men had sufficient intelligence, and that subsequent evolution was primarily in social organization and in the efficiency of cultural exchange and inheritance.

Tools as Adaptive Novelties

As hunting proficiency increased, many other human traits arose. In the cataloguing of man in the previous chapter, we listed several innovations arising during primate and hominid evolution. A partial list of other adaptations whose needs will now be more obvious follows:

(1) The earlier primates, which were plant-eaters, gave rise to meat-eaters when hunting began. Once out of the forest, with fewer plants available, primates were forced to change their diet.

(2) Meat-eating necessitated drastic adaptations in the anatomy of the mouth, teeth, and jaws. Meat is swallowed quickly, then digested internally by enzymes; but plants are chewed, as by a hungry cow, for long periods. There results a need for a different tooth surface in meat-eaters.

Incidentally, man is the only existing primate who is carnivorous. He is not a herbivore anatomically. The only reason he can eat plants is that he has evolved the ability to use fire, and can cook his plants. The cooking digests, or breaks down, the outer coatings of plant cells, a process that the human digestive system is unable to do efficiently. Hence man is called an omnivore, but he is biologically a carnivore. Only culturally is he omnivorous.

(3) As pre-man became carnivorous, he needed to track down the moving targets that could contribute to his hunting trophies. If these animals mi-

grated, as often forced to by glacier movements during the Pleistocene Ice Ages, he had to follow them. Thus did man learn to migrate, occasionally to find more fertile hunting grounds and remain there. He would then become more and more different, by the gradual accumulation of genetic change, than those left behind, perhaps continents away. Sometimes he was literally "trapped" on a new land by the results of the Ice Ages, such as newly formed desert areas, rivers, altered sea levels, and so on. Early *Homo sapiens* was indeed a nomad, moving north and south with the glaciers, in constant search for food and adequate shelter.

The fossil record of pre-man and early man is well dispersed throughout Europe, Asia, and Africa. But there are no fossil finds of hominids in the New World prior to 40,000 years ago, at which time pre-men migrated to North America via Beringia, the Bering land bridge 400 miles wide that connects Asia to Alaska; it is now covered by sea waters, but was exposed by the lowered sea levels of the Wisconsin Ice Age. By 10,000 years ago, man might have been living throughout New England in America, except at its northernmost tip, where some remnants of ice remained. His first appearance in South America occurred between 14,000 and 22,000 years ago.

Obviously then, most of human evolution occurred in the Old World. But did all members of *Homo sapiens sapiens* originate from one stock? If so, did that stock originate in Europe, Asia, or Africa? Or were there several migrated stocks of premen dispersed through the Old World that later independently evolved the necessary anatomies and behaviors to become man? More authors agree that man evolved from one stock, probably in sub-tropical Africa. But others disagree. What confuses the picture is the scarcity of the fossil record, added to the fact that migrations have obscured the hereditary relationships of prehuman stocks.

(4) The increased locomotion and speed of pre-men also increased the need to release excess body heat. This was achieved mainly by evaporation from sweat glands. But body hair prevents, or slows down, profuse evaporation. This is perhaps the most likely reason why *Homo erectus* became a "naked ape."

(5) A good hunt requires communication between members of the hunting party. This is perhaps the need to which we owe our ability to speak. There must have been very powerful selection pressure for communication, first as simple call signals (a particular grunt meaning "Over here"; another "Look out"; another "You go that way, I'll go this way"; another "It's my deer"; etc.). Later, as the mouth became smaller, with less bulky teeth and retracted jaws, it became freer to do things other than to carry, grasp, or bite; in association with correspondingly evolving brain structures, the jaw enabled man to utter more refined sounds and groups of sounds denoting more complex meanings, such as "Now, where should we look tomorrow?"

(6) Pre-man soon learned to strike the enemy with a sharp blow using a tool other than his limbs. A stone, or a bone, was sufficient and more effective. Man, it is said, out-evolved his relatives partly because nature selected the aggression and intelligence which compelled him to use bones to kill the enemy. In South Africa, one fossil find yielded

forty-two prehistoric baboon skulls, each with holes that fitted the indentations which could be made with the thigh bones of small antelopes.

(7) Tool using, first found from sites 2 million years old, and later tool making, caused a further increase in proficiency, improving manual usage and skills. Fire, another culturally significant innovation, is first ascribed to Peking Man, a form of *Homo erectus,* in the mid-Pleistocene. The first human culture is arbitrarily defined by the anthropologist as the origin of *making* crude tools out of pebbles. Succeeding cultures are defined and named according to the types of tools made.

(8) The need for more food and comfort led to more efficient tools, for arrowheads, spears, basins, knives, and so on. Different cultures evolved successively, each more elaborate, each requiring more talent and greater adaptability than the previous.

The above story represents an oversimplified and theoretical path of human evolution. It may be correct, or it may be largely incorrect. But based on all the evidence thus far accumulated, it appears that it is certainly not false; rather it is probably correct, but with modification.

The science of physical anthropology is very young, as is man, and is in a high state of flux. Yet it has progressed rapidly within the past decade, as more and more researches are being initiated, and as dating techniques are being improved. We may, after all, some day know our history as we know ourselves.

XVIII

Tales That Skulls Can Tell

It is possible to deduce many of the life patterns of fossil men by a careful analysis of their bones. Most deductions are based on principles of anatomy and structure.

Let us briefly survey some of these principles.

A bipedal organism that must crouch when it walks or runs is forced to do so because it has a curved thighbone. The less the curvature, the more erect an animal can stand.

The shoulder blade has a cavity, the glenoid cavity, where it joins with other bones; the location and structure of this cavity depends partly upon the type of locomotion of the animal—four-legged, brachiating, or two-legged.

The shape of the pelvis depends upon the extent of erectness of an animal: the shorter and wider the pelvis, the more erect a biped can stand comfortably because the wide pelvis can serve as a "cup" more efficiently. If the pelvis is elongated, or stretched out, it is not as adequate for organ support, although it may be more adequate for the attachment of muscles which give greater strength to the legs.

If limbs are used for locomotion, they tend to become longer in time. For example, brachiators have longer fore-limbs than hindlimbs. Natural selection favors the longer limb because it can increase the speed of a brachiator as it moves through the trees.

The hand and its digits are also subjected to natural selection depending on their functions. Such functions can be deduced in part, for example, from the ratio of thumb length to hand length. This ratio is greatest for man, who uses his thumb for many and diverse functions.

As a final example, some diseases of teeth leave perma-nent and identifiable marks. For example, we deduce from his teeth that one individual *Australopithecus* suffered from a disease due to malnutrition, with attacks at about the ages of two, four, and four and one-half.

The Literature of Skulls

In the family album of the next chapter, we will see a progressive decrease in brow ridges, and in the size of canine teeth. There will also be evident: (1) a progressive forward movement of the anterior part of the skull to accommodate the growing forebrain, and (2) displace-ment of the point of attachment of the spine to the skull, a trait already mentioned. Figure 34 displays this increas-ingly forward alignment for five ancestors of man, and for man himself. In man we see that the skull weight is nearly evenly distributed, front to back, upon the supporting spine. This is less so in Neanderthal man, whose skull was slightly forward of the spine.

Incidentally, a second consequence of a reduced need

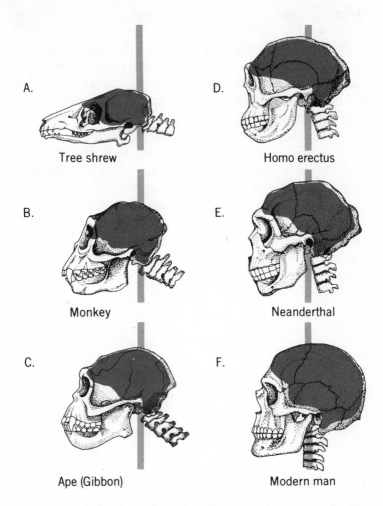

A. Tree shrew

B. Monkey

C. Ape (Gibbon)

D. Homo erectus

E. Neanderthal

F. Modern man

Figure 34. Skulls of primates aligned on pivoting points, showing progressive improvement in balancing. (A) a shrew, (B) a monkey, (C) an ape, (D) Homo erectus, (E) Neanderthal man, (F) modern man.

to support the skull in modern man, besides the ability to produce speech, is that the neck also becomes more flexible; it is able to turn to and fro more rapidly, with the resulting adaptive benefits, especially greater alertness and awareness of one's environment.

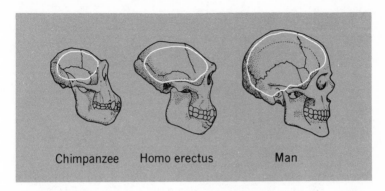

Chimpanzee   Homo erectus   Man

Figure 35. Ratio of brain to face. The brain gets bigger and the face gets smaller, from chimpanzee, Homo erectus, to modern man.

Another tale told by skulls involves the ratio of *brain space* to *face*. As seen in Figure 35, and as would logically be expected, the small brained chimpanzee must rely largely on his jaws for survival; more so than the larger brained *Homo erectus,* and even more so than the still larger brained *Homo sapiens*. Obviously, as the brain case became larger, the face portion of the skull became smaller.

Therefore, as it is for other bones, many skull traits help to indicate the owner's abilities and mode of life. For another example, as intelligence increased, and as animals found better means to protect themselves, skull thickness decreased, as did the need for bulky brow ridges for protection of the eyes and for chewing. We can say with reasonable certainty that the larger the brain, the thinner need be the walls of the primate skull. Also, the more an animal uses its jaws to catch and bite and tear and crush, the stronger must the skull be; this is then partly why the gorilla skull bones of Figure 36 are much thicker than the

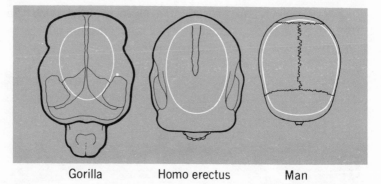

Gorilla   Homo erectus   Man

Figure 36. Skulls of gorilla, Homo erectus, modern man, showing decreasing thickness of skull bones and lessened jutting of jaws. The hatched areas represent brain space.

human skull bones. *Homo erectus* represents an intermediate stage.

It is also probably true that as the need to bite and chew decreases, the chewing apparatus, which as stated before includes the brow ridges working with the upper jaw in a solid framework, is reduced. This leads to a decrease in the jutting out of the jaw. Consequently, as the jaw lightens and the teeth become smaller, there is more space for other things. And as the skull thins out, there is more space for brain tissue.

What is strikingly evident from the above is the fact that several traits develop together, if they are all adapting the organism for the same function. The many skull modifications aimed at producing man, with the thinner brain case, receded jaw, forward forehead, speech apparatus, larger brain, etc., cannot be listed in order of occurrence, since there is no such order; or if there is, there is so much overlap that we cannot possibly specify when it was that one trait made another trait possible.

The process of change is very slow and erratic. We must not imagine that as a forebrain enlarged, it became so large that it pushed the forehead outward; not so. All of the evolutionarily beneficial processes occurred gradually, overlapping each other, and reinforcing one another. It is usually not a case of "Which came first, the chicken or the egg?", but instead, "How did the chicken and the egg work together to make possible such and such a function?"

Skull Indexes

"Skull men" have devised several methods for measuring accurately the various dimensions of skulls to provide comparative data. Some of these indexes are described below.

(1) *Index of cephalization.* It is not always meaningful to compare the brain sizes of various fossil men. It is not sufficient to point to the gradual increase in brain volume from pre-men to man, since man is bigger than were the pre-men. Although several authors of basic textbooks on evolution do not point this out, it seems that there must be some accounting for body size. Of course a three-foot animal has a smaller brain than a six-foot man. The index of cephalization takes into account body weight by determining the ratio of brain weight to body weight. It is greatest for man, and least for mammals other than primates.

(2) *Condyle position index.* The spine makes contact with the skull, to support it, at two protrusions called condyles. This index measures the extent to which this point of contact is centralized beneath the skull. In Figure 37, the ratio of the length of line CD to line EC is an indication of how well the skull is supported. The more forword point C is, generally speaking, the less the musculature needed to help support the skull.

(3) *Supra-orbit height index.* This measures the size of the skull vault, that part above the level of the orbits. It

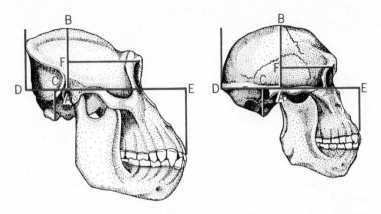

Figure 37. Skulls of (A) an ape, and (B) Australopithecus, showing lines used to calculate skull indexes.

gives an indication of the amount of actual brain space
available in a skull. In Figure 37, the ratio of line FB to
line FA provides the index. The longer FB is compared
with FA, the more brain space there is. Interestingly, this
value increases gradually and consistently from early pre-
men to modern man.

(4) *Nasal index.* The reason that the nose has become
such a prominent and large feature on our faces is not to
assist the sense of smell. Instead, its size is proportional
to the humidity of the air in the region men inhabited as
they evolved. The tropical nose is more flat and open, and
in dry areas it is bigger and more closed. This difference
is due to the fact that, besides smelling, the nose filters,
warms, and *moistens* the air that enters through it. In a
dry area, therefore, there has evolved a nose more capable
of moistening the dry air entering. The nasal index gives
an indication of the relative shape of skull nasal openings.

(5) There is also an index to measure the extent of
jutting out of the jaws, relative to the rest of the skull. In

our ancestral line, it is least in modern man, most in early pre-men.

(6) The number of teeth, and the number of elevations on some teeth, are indicative of the type of diet, the means of acquiring food, and the mode of self-protection in primate animals.

There are many other measurements made on fossil skulls. Pieced together, they provide information that can help either to corroborate or to deny the theories of how pre-men lived, how they adapted, how they fit into the scheme of human evolution.

XIX

A Family Album

Imagine that you are faced with four Chevrolets, a 1960, a 1961, a 1962, and a 1963. They are all stripped completely of their outer surfaces and of all inner structures that were perishable. The only remains you can see, separated and buried, some deeply embedded into rock, are: the wheels of each car, the four engines largely disassembled, a few other metal parts such as a couple of rods, bits and pieces of a muffler, and an ashtray with gum and ashes in it. There are also three lollipop sticks, a few leather soles, a hat, a St. Christopher medal.

You are then asked to put them together as they were originally, to determine the sequence in which they were produced within those four years, and to tell something of the mode of life of their owners.

Besides the obvious difficulties exposed, the above also illustrates that there *is* a proper sequence; there *were* four successive automobiles called the 1961, the 1962, and so on. But only an expert could reconstruct the past from such evidence with some degree of accuracy.

Similarly fossil bones and tools can relate a story to an expert—one that becomes more and more credible as more and more bones and tools fall into place. But we must hurry. Even as our detective work is improving, the Earth is moving. The longer we wait, the less likely will be the culmination of fossil knowledge. Deeper and deeper, and more and more fragmented, become the bones man seeks so diligently and so strenuously, as if in search of long lost loved ones.

Perhaps man needs now to know himself more than ever before. To know himself, he must first know where he came from. Knowledge of the present is only partial knowledge; unfounded knowledge. In this mission only the anthropologist can help, for only he has the training and ability to extract from a simple jaw bone, or a tooth, thousands of years of history.

One startling property of existence that I hope stood out as we surveyed the process of human and pre-human evolution is that it is as difficult to define "man" in his transitional stages as it is to define life or matter, or to differentiate between the simplest plants and animals, or between life and death at their borderline. It is very simple to tell a man from a shrew today; or a man from an ape or a monkey. But as we travel further into the past, we find them looking and acting more and more alike. Polarization; an outcome of evolution discussed in Chapter V and evident throughout this book.

At in-between, transitional stages, whatever definitions we apply will not affect reality, will not affect what things really are or were. But our definitions can and do affect our quest for knowledge, hence affect the path of future evolution as we help to determine it. We must often be arbitrary in our definitions and categorizations, but we must realize that we are being arbitrary.

A Family Album

I wish at this time to introduce to you some of the pre-men who have figured heavily in the evolutionary process that yielded this writer and you, the reader, today.

Proconsul

A Miocene primate from East Africa. He appeared 25 million years ago. The first ground anthropoid ape, he was three feet tall, could stand upright, but usually walked on all fours. He displayed extreme jutting of the jaws, a greatly receded forehead, a massive lower jaw, no brow ridge, a dense hairy coat, and an opposable thumb. His huge canine teeth indicate that he had no defensive tools, but instead would bite an attacker. As a four-legged animal whose skeleton is intermediate between those of future brachiators and two-legged forms, he could have been the stem from which they evolved, from which evolved the apes and pre-men.

He was diurnal, sleeping at night, because his sense of smell left much to be desired, and he had developed a color vision useful primarily in daylight. It is thought that at first, *Proconsul* was lightly pigmented, due to the low intensity of light in the dense forests in which he originated. Gradually however, as later generations left the forests, there probably developed a heavy pigmentation in naked parts of the skin, especially the face, to prevent overproduction of vitamin D. He organized social groupings with a dominance hierarchy and established a kind

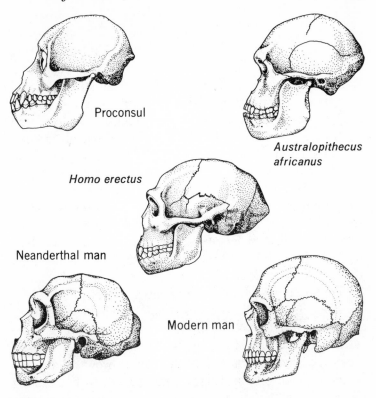

Figure 38. Skulls of Proconsul, *Australopithecus africanus*, *Homo erectus*, Neanderthal man, and Modern man.

of territoriality in which he retreated to the center of an established territory; only the dominant males ventured out to the edge of the territory to prevent entry to foreigners.

Australopithecus africanus

First discovered in 1924 in South Africa, this pre-man appears to be a man from the neck down, and an ape from the neck up. He stood erect, as evidenced partly from the "lumbar curve" of his spine, weighed from 60 to 120 pounds, was about four feet tall, and probably had black skin. He may have arisen as early as 5½ million years ago. Canine teeth were further reduced, but he still displayed considerable jaw jutting. Brow ridges were also considerably reduced, indicating a keener mind and a decreased need to bite or chew. He had a higher forehead, indicating an enlarging brain. The skull was better aligned upon the spine than in apes, and this required fewer muscles to support the jaw, indicating that he could exercise greater freedom of movement in his jaws, perhaps even for simple speech. In fact, it is speculated that he may have used some basic form of language. He may have used pebbles for tools, and did use broken bones to kill. It is assumed that in periods of drought, or lack of food, he began to form a family structure; this was advantageous in dividing the band into smaller groups, some of whom were more likely to survive than if they had to share food and water with a greater number. He had a more robust cousin, *Australopithecus robustus*, with heavier brow ridges, and a funny looking bony ridge running front to back along the top of his skull. This cousin weighed in at 140 pounds and was a vegetarian. He did not have the necessary anatomy to proceed to humanlike status, but *Australopithecus africanus* did.

Piltdown Man

A fraud. A very clever and intentional fraud whose ramifications in the field of anthropology extended from 1908 to 1953. Combining human skull fragments with the jawbone and teeth of some apes, some joker buried them some distance apart in a gravel pit near the eastern coast of England. The bones had been filed down and treated with chemicals to make them appear to be fossilized. An unsuspecting British lawyer and amateur archeologist "discovered" the bones in 1909 and, with the expert opinion of a geologist, announced the find in 1912.

> There is little reason for doubting that the Piltdown man lived near the beginning of the glacial period or at the end of the preceding period. His age is estimated from 200,000 years to a million years.

> Although we know nothing of the bodily skeletal characters of the Piltdown woman, we are safe in assuming at least that she was an erect walker with a fully human foot.

So wrote an unsuspecting Dr. Ernest Hooton of Harvard University, in his 1931 book *Up from the Ape*.

And Dr. Richard Lull of Yale University had written in *The Evolution of Earth and Man*, 1929:

> The matter has . . . been settled beyond question by the finding of a second specimen of the Piltdown man some two miles distant, . . .

Piltdown caused considerable blushing, and serves as a thorn in the side of scientific progress; a humiliation. But perhaps the most beneficial of all "fossil" finds has been that of the nonexisting Piltdown man. Since it placed anthropologists on an eternal guard, there has resulted an extreme caution in the categorizing of fossil finds. This is the main reason for the lack of conformity and agreement among modern anthropologists. The reason there have been so many names for different fossil men is possibly because few anthropologists agree on the final decision:

where does fossil X or fossil Y belong in our family tree?

Piltdown is a fraud to which we owe much of our present and future progress in the search for pre-man.

Homo erectus

A small erect carnivore, sixty pounds heavy and five and one-half feet tall, very closely allied to man, he had a significantly larger brain than *Australopithecus*. Initially, he was more heavily pigmented than *Proconsul* had become; and he had less pronounced jaws but thicker brow ridges than *Australopithecus africanus*. He arrived around one million years ago, and extended tool-making greatly; one form, Peking man, used fire to roast his animals. Peking man was a cannibal, enlarging the holes in animal skulls to extract the edible brain. *Erectus* was a more or less naked hominid, and it is assumed that he was capable of speech, hence he may have developed languages, certainly much beyond any that *Australopithecus africanus* might have had. Possibly it was nakedness that brought about the first use of fire. *Erectus* migrated, and some forms adapted to zones far removed from the tropics. On a chilly night, one's muscles are compelled to shiver, to produce the body heat necessary to compensate for the cold. Under such conditions, there must have been strong selection pressures for shivering and for the use of fire. Such may also have been the stimulus to the extensive use of animal skins for clothing. *Erectus*, it is assumed by some anthropologists, formed "races," so that Peking man (bronze-yellow), Heidelberg man (white), and the original *erectus* populations (black) adapted their skin pigmentations to the geographic latitude at which they finally settled. The subject is far from clear at this time.

Homo sapiens neanderthalensis

The first fossil find ever identified as an ancestor of man was of this chap, who was found in Germany in 1856. He existed about 150,000 years ago, possibly but not necessarily from a "race" of *Homo erectus.* He was white, very muscular and bony, and about five feet tall. His jaws jutted out significantly less than did those in *Homo erectus,* but still more than in modern man. He had a higher forehead, and orbits still protected by brow ridges, although the latter were smaller than in *Homo erectus.* The lower jaw was much thinner than in *Homo erectus,* indicating that he had specialized in artificial means to kill his prey and to cook his foods. Stone tools, including knives, scrapers, borers, and saws, have been found with his remains. He dressed in furs and migrated south in winter. He had a well-organized culture and society. He was even perhaps somewhat "philosophical" about death, as evidenced by the careful and ceremonial burying of his corpses 70,000 years ago.

He disappeared 40,000 years ago; it is uncertain whether (1) he was a race of pre-man living at the same time as other pre-men were evolving elsewhere, (2) he was "lost" by hybridization with other pre-men, by intermarrying with other local "races," or (3) he himself evolved into modern man, by gradual change. He was soon followed, in an evolutionary sense, by Cro-Magnon man, whose paintings we find on cave walls from as early as 30,000 years ago.

Homo sapiens sapiens

The most advanced stage of hominid evolution is *Homo sapiens*. His brain volume has increased by 40 percent in the past 600,000 years, and by 47 percent in the 300,000 years before that. But as "modern man," he originated 40,000 years ago. He has a well-established society, with a dominance hierarchy. His forehead is nearly vertical, due to an advancing forebrain, and brow ridges are nearly absent, as is jaw jutting. The skull is nearly, but not quite centrally aligned atop the spine. Of 1,500,000 known animal species, he is the only one able to write and to read books on evolution. Of 193 surviving species of monkeys and apes, he is the only one naked, unencumbered with hair or fur. He represents a stage where nature has finally achieved a product able to plan and control future natural selection, by applying artificial selection pressure.

XX

The Future: Who'll Run the Show?

Man has evolved from the animals. He is still an instinctive animal, but only partly so. He is in the process of polarizing, of diverging from other animals. He is becoming increasingly able to utilize his intelligence to suppress his instincts.

But he is not yet perfect. He is not even near perfection.

How Man Is Imperfect

Man's biology could improve markedly. His anatomy contains many structures that he cannot use, and others that wear out rather early. His gene pool contains many defective genes. His health and his resistance to disease are in dire need of improvement.

The many mental derangements manifested in the human species are another imperfection. Many of these disorders are being propagated, and at alarming rates.

Further, if we study the intelligence aspect of man, it becomes clear that the average I.Q. is far below that which we would call perfect. The fact that there are I.Q.s above the average range of 90 to 110 shows that this range is not the potential of which man is capable. Also, intelligence quotients from 0 to 90 still exist in abundant numbers, producing children and adults sadly unable to take care of themselves.

Man's sociological aspect is also in need of improvement, as is obvious from studies of crime, deviant sex, lack of love and compassion, and excesses of pride, hate, selfishness, and social prejudice.

This leads to a question: since man rests on the evolutionary ladder, and since man is not yet a fully adapted species, will he ever become so? Is evolution at a dead end (poor choice of words) in our line, or is it still in progress?

It would be unwarranted to assume that the modern human being represents the end of the process of primate evolution. Instead, it seems obvious that subsequent human evolution will be psycho-social, rather than biological. Man's intellect and his social organization will probably continue their adaptation. That is, of course, as long as the environment does not change more rapidly than we can adapt to it. If a natural, or a man-caused, change in world temperature, atmospheric makeup, or in abundance of oxygen-producing plants occurs, we could be as doomed as were the dinosaurs, even with our intelligence.

But I am not of the pessimist school. I trust in man. He is very resilient, and adaptive. He will survive, barring unforeseen *natural* disasters. But meanwhile, he faces several problems.

People Are People Are More People

Perhaps the most critical questions related to the future of *Homo sapiens* are these. (1) Will he be able to utilize psycho-social means to control his rapidly expanding population, before his built-in biological checks do so automatically? (2) Will he be able to develop means of genetic improvement before the onset of irreversible genetic deterioration? Let us survey the first question.

The total mass of man is now 200 million tons. There are 10 billion cubic feet of people on the Earth.

Many of us detest such inhuman statistical references to mankind, and well we should; people should mean more to us, on a daily-and-downtown basis, than their weight or volume.

But we just cannot forget that the anatomy of man must be fed. There is no escape from this fact. And what he eats is food; he eats food to get the energy his cells need to live. This energy comes from green plants, and comes ultimately from the sun. Simple facts, simple logic.

Now, another simple fact: the sun lets our planet have just so much of its energy, and no more. If too many people eat too much something will have to give, somewhere. The Earth, another simple fact, can hold only so much living stuff, be it in plants, worms, people, or any combination of these.

Before the agricultural revolution, the human population reached a peak and probably could not have increased further without detrimental effect. Another, higher peak was reached after the agricultural revolution; and still a higher level after the industrial revolution. And we cannot deny the feasibility of other revolutions in food production; in fact, the hybridization of wheat and other plants may represent the beginning of another revolution, the Green Revolution.

Some speculate that the Earth might be "good" for 10 billion people, others go as high as 90 billion or more. But, as is true of all living things, any population of a species lives in a habitat that has a limited *carrying capacity*. Any plot of land, or water, can provide only so much food and energy. Sooner or later man will run out of revolutions, and of food. If he can find an alternate source, he may survive; but it seems unlikely that he will find such. It seems improbable that man can exceed his *optimal population level* and survive to write about it.

There have been many studies to determine how other animals control their population sizes instinctively. In overcrowded conditions, fruit flies merely reduce the rate of egg-laying; flower beetles resort to cannibalism, or release a gas lethal to their babies; chickens suffer a fatal heart disease; chipmunk females wean their young too soon and kick them out of the burrow, probably to be eaten by owls or snakes; snowshoe rabbits have heart attacks, or their wombs abort the fetuses.

Rats respond to overcrowding in strange ways. Some experiments have shown them to become oversexual, homosexual, and cannibalistic. Further, if given a choice after being exposed to long-term overcrowding, they prefer to remain crowded. But when in the crowd, they remain aloof, uninvolved, and alone. It is interesting, but frightening, to attempt to relate this to life in man's megalopolis.

The animal body, it was found, increases the production of some hormones when the number of bumps, contacts with others, reaches a certain value. We have all experienced instinctive frustration when pushed around too much, too many times in rapid succession. We become angry and cannot halt the speech or elbowing that may result.

There appears to have evolved in man some very definite biological responses to crowding. Boredom causes a change in brain wave patterns—the significance is not yet known—compared with records from an active person. Depression precedes, and may possibly bring about, several diseases, perhaps at times even hepatitis or pancreatic ulcers. Anxiety can cause diarrhea, constipation, or abnormal digestion. An exaggerated need for a mother figure can cause asthma. Stress can cause nasal discharge, sore throat, or deafness. Ulcers; sweating; coronary distress; respiratory ailments. The list seems endless.

If, as seems evident, overcrowding and its resulting economic and social pressures can cause depression, anxiety, and stress, then perhaps the real effect of overpopulation in psycho-social man will be felt locally, by people, by you and me, before the onset of world famine, pestilence, or war.

To be sure, there are results of overpopulation that affect whole masses of people, such as the 500,000 residents of Pakistan who died in November of 1970 because of a cyclone—these people were forced to live in a perilous region just above sea level, forced there because there were too many other people elsewhere in the land.

But the twentieth-century population increase, with resulting mechanical and economic revolutions, is causing difficulties other than statistical; difficulties often detrimental to our intellect as well as to our biology; ambiguous, uncomfortable, subtle difficulties. Local and personal difficulties. It is not sufficient to fear famine and epidemic. The peril could be much more immediate. The very core of human psychology is threatened with a suicidal invasion of privacy when one desires privacy, complemented with a pitiless rejection of personal sharing when one wishes to share. Not always true, but probably more true now than ever before.

The answer? Man need not fear the consequences of overpopulation as long as he fears the consequences of overpopulation. This bit of doubletalk can be translated thusly: there is no question but that man's population is approaching perilous levels, and there are three possible solutions. (1) He will become extinct for lack of food or by other destructive means. (2) He will reduce and/or reverse the rate of increase by becoming psycho-socially aware he must do something. (3) His biology will be able to apply the built-in checks to overpopulation, checks that are a part of his inheritance, that work by gnawing at his health and psychological stability.

He will probably apply number 2. As long as he realizes that there is a problem, he will solve it. Fear not for man, for he is evolving, inventive, and desirous of survival.

Can Man, Should Man, Improve His Genes?

The field of medicine has permitted many of us to live who surely would have been selected against by natural selection, if we were of another species or of pre-medicine times. As a result, the gene pool of man is rapidly accumulating inferior genes. Genes are being passed on that would not be in nature.

Now I use the word "inferior" here solely to designate those genes that cause such things as severe deformity, severe retardation, severe antisocial behavior, and so on; conditions that most of us would admit are pitiful, and should be corrected. Some refer to fit and unfit people; I prefer to omit here the discussion of social norms, and to refer only to conditions commonly accepted as very unfortunate.

We must realize that man is becoming a major component of Mother Nature. He is permitting to live many who would ordinarily die before they reach the age of reproduction.

If we look at the gene pool of man it is obvious, as has been shown by countless studies, that the frequency of detrimental genes is increasing; this must mean that the frequency of beneficial genes is decreasing. But what can we do about it? We certainly have a right to detest forced sterilization of mental defectives or criminals; we can reject any measure that would prevent someone from reproducing, or that would deny a medical cure to someone who wishes it.

But we also have a right to seek cures for the present genetic breakdown of mankind. Very many social and biological proposals have been made for the genetic improvement of man. Some are sound and humane; others are pitiless and undemocratic. For further reading, the works of Francis Galton, Herman Muller, Julian Huxley, and Garrett Hardin are suggested.

In addition to the eugenic measures for human betterment, measures that resort to such practices as artificial insemination and sterilization, there are also the consequences of Genetic Engineering, the proposals for attacking the inferior genes themselves, instead of their owners, people. This would be more likely to become accepted as standard procedure, if we ever become able to implement it, but at this time we are still unable to do so. Research has not yet produced gene surgery for higher animals.

But the field of Genetic Engineering, which consists of the attempt to learn more about human or animal gene structures and operations and how to manipulate them, has come a long way based mostly on work with bacteria and viruses, and with single cells from higher animals and plants.

We can now remove the hereditary material of a virus

and inject it into the cells of other organisms. We can transform one type of human cell into another type. We can perform genetic surgery in small organisms; that involves, for example, the transfer of genes from one type of bacterium to another. The imposed change can then be passed on, from one generation to the next. We can produce simple genetic messages and use them in such transformation experiments.

In *Science,* December 18, 1970 ("Prospects for Genetic Intervention in Man"), Dr. Bernard Davis wrote that ". . . the isolation of human genes . . . may also be accomplished quite soon. . . . We would then be able to synthesize and to modify human genes in the test tube." Dr. Marshall Nirenberg, of the National Heart Institute, wrote in August of 1967: "My guess is that cells will be programmed with synthetic messages within 25 years."

Let us review some specific laboratory findings. Perhaps the first experiment in gene transformation (artificial change in a gene to cause it to perform differently, hence to cause the cell or organ of which it is a part to perform differently) was done in 1944. Then, nearly thirty years ago, genetic material from a calf's thymus gland was given to a fruit fly, and brought about predictable changes in the fly's appearance. In 1965, a virus known as SV 40 was used to transform one type of human cell into another very different type by two Russian scientists. SV 40 has been used extensively ever since, in other experiments.

In the last five years, results have been truly astounding. The use of virus hereditary material seems to have no limit. Other viruses have been used, and the number is increasing. In October of 1969, a report in *Science* described the first permanent genetic change in an isolated human cell brought about by completely purified DNA. The day of specific and desired change is near.

Of assistance to the researcher is the cell culture technique that allows him to isolate human cells—heart, skin, cancer cells, for example—and keep them alive indefinitely. And the cells continue to multiply; one cell can yield a million cells in four weeks. The transfer of a cell nucleus is also possible, by micro-surgery. The nucleus of one type of animal or plant cell can be removed and replaced by the nucleus from another type, and the former cell becomes transformed. In fact, a preliminary study has even combined mouse and human hereditary materials to form a temporary "mouse-human" cell.

Based on such achievements, what might one expect in the future? That depends on whether you mean the near or the distant future. It is utterly useless to predict too far in advance. But in principle, any human trait will surely become subject to genetic transformation, if it is genetically caused. In practice however, the methods of genetic surgery will probably be applied only to alleviate inherited defects.

But may we, must we, change a gene pool that is to become the ancestor of future gene pools? May we establish goals for future generations? Of course we may. Since we have no choice but to be the descendants of other generations, since it is our gene pool, and ours alone, that we will pass on, then we have a double responsibility: we must ensure ourselves an adequate gene pool, and we must safeguard it for our children's children.

How Can Man Affect the Evolution of Nature?

By being alive, and by being man, we affect nature in its evolving process by nearly everything we do. But that is true of all other organisms; everything they do affects their environment as well.

But we can do more, and do it faster and over a wider range. Aye, there's the rub!

But we need not leave nature alone. Every living thing exploits its environment to survive; why not man? We must build houses and dams. The question is where, how, and how many? We must kill carrots and pigs; but without disrupting the evolved ecological balance.

Foxes eat rabbits, so you might say that foxes disrupt the balance. But this is partly how the two species have evolved to check their respective population sizes. This is *part* of the balance. When the rabbit population is too low, foxes die, and their population decreases; this enables the rabbit population to increase, only to cause an increase in fox population, and so on.

But man is different. He controls his own population by social and cultural means. He is learning; he is young; he will most probably survive. But while he learns he can make an awful pest of himself! Take only one example, the pastime called hunting.

Hunting may have been completely necessary for the survival of pre-man and early man. But since the pilgrims brought their muskets over, at least twenty-two species of mammals, birds, and fishes have become extinct. Extinct! Gone. No more. Evolved into oblivion. Most probably never to evolve again. And still, even if sixty other species, at the very least, are in extreme danger of the same fate, man hunts.

It is interesting how human nature permits us to kill some animals and not others. And the reasons are sometimes strange. We care not about stepping on an ant, swatting a fly, carving a sharp hook into the top of a fish mouth, or deliberately filling a deer's head with lead. But we are ready to pound to the ground anyone who drowns a cat, carelessly drives over a dog, or just for kicks ties the tails of a couple of hamsters together.

We care not if nice little Johnny leaves a green frog to dehydrate in a pail in the backyard. We will cut worms in four or five pieces for bait, but we wish to kill the fisherman who does not throw the undersized catch back into the pond.

Perhaps man likes to kill large animals because it gives him a subconscious sense of dominance. It could be a remnant of his cave days. The week with the boys, with camper, beer, fishing pole, and rifle, could be an instinctive excuse to revert to hominid days.

I have killed animals too, being a biologist. I have always preferred to call my acts sacrifices, however. I like to think that when my students sacrifice a rat, lobster, or frog, they are gaining experience needed for their future in medicine and the biological sciences.

I have never once seen a student leave the laboratory with his earthworm or dogfish proudly displayed on top of a car.

The End of the Beginning

The evolution of man is the first evolution to be observed and recorded. And although I have "knocked" some of man's childish attributes and pranks, I hope to have impressed upon the reader that this product of 4.8 billion years of evolution is to be respected and honored and safeguarded as no other product is.

But to do those things, we must first realize that man is both an animal and not an animal. If we allow our pride to deny that we are still largely instinctive, then we will never learn to supersede the animal in man. On the other hand, if we permit our instincts to overcome our intelligence, then we will never evolve into a better human animal.

As far as nature and its ecology are concerned, man is a Thing, as is a screwdriver, a dog, a lamp, a highway system, a frog. But man has the potential to overcome nature, to guide it, to improve it, to destroy it. Since he still depends on nature for his very survival, he must not destroy it, but must evolve along with it; adapting it no faster than it can adapt, destroying it no faster than it can heal itself.

Not only is nature worthy of the highest respect, but so is man worthy of the cost of genetic improvement, of social integration and coordination, and of the higher than highest respect. The polarization that he instills, as all other living and non-living Things instill, must be an integrated and coordinated polarization, a getting along of different factions. But it need not be a complete merger of the different factions; plants and animals need not become alike; life and chemicals need not become alike; human whites and blacks need not become biologically alike, but socially equal.

The evolved nature thrives on differences; but only if the different parts continue to evolve and cooperate for the common good.

Perhaps a closing poem is due, in honor of nature, of life, and of man and his evolving society.

> Clouds of starlight sprinkling faintly
>   night's cavernous shadow
> Clouds of mist abiding discreetly
>   dusk's evasive meadow
> Clouds of sparrows clinging tightly
>   'bove Earth's menagerie
> Clouds of electrons spinning webs
>   'neath nature's privacy.

The realm of nature has an awesome perplexity.
In daily transfusions we imbibe its simplicity,
In enchanting confusions we measure its immensity.

To be in nature; to remain in nature.
To live, not to die.
But alas we must die.
So others may live. So others may pry.

A Suggested Reading Program

There are very many good books on the various aspects of the topic of evolution. A few are listed below. These have been selected for their general excellence and interest for the general reader.

The reader who wishes to pursue this topic further would profit most from the reading of all twelve works listed, and in the order listed.

(1) *The Universe: From Flat Earth to Quasar.* By Isaac Asimov. Avon Books, 1966.

(2) *The Age of Dinosaurs.* By Bjorn Kurten. McGraw-Hill Book Company, 1968.

(3) *Mimicry in Plants and Animals.* By Wolfgang Wickler. McGraw-Hill Book Company, 1968.

(4) *On Aggression.* By Konrad Lorenz. Bantam Books, 1970.

(5) *The Emergence of Man.* By John E. Pfeiffer. Harper & Row, Publishers, 1970.

(6) *Man and the Environment: An Introduction to Human Ecology and Evolution.* By Arthur S. Boughey. The Macmillan Company, 1971.

(7) *Race and Races.* By Richard A. Goldsby. The Macmillan Company, 1971.

(8) *Science, Conflict, and Society*. Reading from *Scientific American*. W. H. Freeman Company, 1969.

(9) *The Biological Time Bomb*. By Gordon R. Taylor. New American Library, 1969.

(10) *Utopian Motherhood: New Trends in Human Reproduction*. By Robert T. Francoeur. Doubleday & Company, Inc., 1970.

(11) *The Population Bomb*. By Paul R. Ehrlich. Ballantine Books, 1968.

Perhaps one of the best introductory textbooks on the topic of biological evolution is:

(12) *Introduction to Evolution*. By Paul A. Moody. Harper & Row, Publishers, 1970.